Everyday
Evangelism

ALSO BY BILLIE HANKS. . .
Discipleship: The Best Writings

Everyday Evangelism

BILLIE HANKS, JR.

ZONDERVAN
PUBLISHING HOUSE
OF THE ZONDERVAN CORPORATION
GRAND RAPIDS, MICHIGAN 49506

EVERYDAY EVANGELISM
Copyright © 1983 by The Zondervan Corporation
Grand Rapids, Michigan

Library of Congress Cataloging in Publication Data

Hanks, Billie.
  Everyday evangelism.

  1. Evangelistic work. 2. Witness bearing (Christian-
ity) I. Title.
BV3790.H337 1983   269'.2   83-13713
ISBN 0-310-44641-4

Edited by Edward Viening
Printed in the United States of America

83 84 85 86 87 88 — 10 9 8 7 6 5 4 3 2 1

*Dedicated to my
Mother and Father,
who have believed and encouraged,*

*and my Sister,
who has been a close
friend on the journey*

Contents

Foreword

One who writes books on evangelism should be acquainted with the subject in at least two ways. First, one should know evangelism theoretically, from the standpoint of its biblical basis, its theology, and its need. But the person who writes most helpfully on evangelism must also be acquainted with the subject experientially. It must be practiced in the life of the writer. Truths about evangelism must be not only in his head but must also be incarnate in his daily experience. It is at this point that Billie Hanks is eminently qualified to write on this subject. The real strength of the book lies in the fact that it has been hammered out in the crucible of experience.

The uniqueness of this book lies in the range of its appeal. It is helpful for the novice or beginner in evangelism. On the other hand, it has a great deal of helpful material for the seasoned veteran.

One strong feature of the book is its emphasis on training someone else to be effective in evangelism. Frequently, the author makes reference to one's "Timothy." A "Timothy" is a person who is being trained by a more experienced Christian. For this reason, the vision of the book extends beyond that of most books on the subject of evangelism. It is not only a "how to" book on evangelism, but also a "how to" book on multiplying the number of evangelizers.

Another helpful aspect of this book is its emphasis on cross-cultural evangelism. Chapter 10, which deals with presenting the gospel to non-Trinitarians, is especially strong. The material on sharing with Jews and Muslims is unique to most books of this type.

I heartily commend this book to you. You will be more prepared to fulfill your part of the Great Commission through reading it.

Roy J. Fish
Professor of Evangelism
Southwestern Baptist Theological Seminary
Fort Worth, Texas

Acknowledgments

When so many friends and loved ones have made an impact on your life, it is difficult to give adequate credit for the numerous insights and blessings that you have received.

My greatest hope is that the reader will understand that the many personal illustrations in these chapters are a direct result of my being a debtor to those who have discipled me. It is my prayer that this book will be used as a tool for training and that many will come to Christ and then be discipled because of its message.

Certain individuals have specifically joined me in that expectation and have helped in making this book become a reality.

I want to express my deepest appreciation to:

Ruth, Heidi, and Heather, for listening again and again to each chapter as the thoughts crystallized.

Bill Shell, for helping me organize the content of the book.

Grady Wilson and each of my Pauls for the valuable training they provided by letting me be a Timothy.

Deonne Beshear and our staff at International Evangelism for many hours of editing and hard work on the manuscript.

Finlay Graham, Earl Martin, and Jim McPherson, for their numerous helpful suggestions related to Islam.

Wayne Watts and I.E.A.'s Board, for their faithful prayers.

And last, but certainly not least, Ed Viening and Zondervan's outstanding staff, for their encouraging spirit and supreme patience.

Introduction

This book is different. The difference is the emphasis on the Paul/Timothy relationship and its modern-day application. It presents evangelism not only as something that you and I must do but as something we must help others to learn to do. We must not only pass on the gospel message, but we must be diligent in teaching others to do the same.

Every convert is a potential evangelist. But more than that, every convert is a potential trainer of evangelists. The objective of our follow-up of new believers is not only to help them become established in the faith but to help them become lifetime laborers in the kingdom of God—producing reproducers. It is this vision of evangelistic multiplication that grips the heart of the reader.

But there's a snag. This vision costs something. It cannot be done by planning a punchy little program, pushing the button, and watching it roll. This ministry is accomplished by people, not programs. Nor can it be done by tossing a person a piece of literature, hoping he or she will follow the directions and get on with the job.

This ministry is accomplished by *someone*, not by *something*. It is accomplished by the person who takes the new babe by the warm hand and leads him through the perils of spiritual infancy and adolescence. It is a person who imparts to him the basics of the Christian walk and witness, helping him to be fruitful and multiply.

The apostle Paul spoke of this in his letter to the Thessalonians: "You are witnesses, and so is God, how devoutly and uprightly and blamelessly we behaved toward you believers; just as you know how we were exhorting and encouraging and imploring each one of you as a father would his own children, so that you may walk in a manner worthy of the God who calls you into His own kingdom and glory" (1 Thess. 2:10-12, NASB).

He compared his relationship with them to that of a father with his child. He did not look upon them as his "contacts." He saw them as his spiritual children, for whom he felt a parental responsibility.

Note the intensity of his words: "But we proved to be gentle among you, as a nursing mother tenderly cares for her own children. Having thus a fond affection for you, we were well-pleased to impart to you not only the gospel of God but also our own lives, because you had become very dear to us" (1 Thess. 2:7,8, NASB).

Paul shared this same relationship with Timothy. It rings loud and clear in his letter to this young man whom he was training to be a lifetime laborer in the kingdom of God.

Note how he describes it to the Philippians: "But I hope in the Lord Jesus to send Timothy to you shortly, so that I also may be encouraged when I learn of your condition. For I have no one else of kindred spirit who will genuinely be concerned for your welfare. For they all seek after their own interests, not those of Christ Jesus. But you know of his proven worth that he served with me in the furtherance of the gospel like a child serving his father" (Phil. 2:19-23, NASB). Timothy had served as a son with his father in the gospel.

Notice Paul's emphasis: "in the gospel." Paul had trained Timothy to do evangelism and in one of his letters to him encouraged him to "do the work of an evangelist." But it was not to stop there. Yes, Paul taught Timothy to witness. But it was not to stop there. He urged Timothy to train others, as well. "And the things which you have heard from me in the presence of many witnesses, these entrust to faithful men, who will be able to teach others also" (2 Tim. 2:2, NASB).

That's one of the great emphases of the book. Yes, we are able to witness. Yes, there are many valuable lessons to help us to do that. But this book brings out another step. If we do our work well, when we have "run with patience the race that is set before us," when we come to the end, there will be others to whom we can pass the torch. If we do our work well, then there will be many who will multiply our ministries of evangelism and training long after we have left the scene.

LeRoy Eims, Assistant to the Pres.
The Navigators
Colorado Springs, Colorado

1

Producing Love for God

Early in my Christian pilgrimage, God used the following passage to motivate me in the ministry of personal evangelism: "And this gospel of the kingdom will be preached in the whole world as a testimony to all nations, and then the end will come" (Matt. 24:14).

One night this statement of Jesus was indelibly impressed upon my heart, and it was then that God confronted me with the truth that evangelism was to be the principal task of my life. Since that time I have grown in my conviction that every person who receives Christ must be shown that evangelism is the foremost concern on the heart of God.

The Objective of Evangelism

The first commandment, "You shall love the Lord your God with all your heart, and with all your soul, and with all your mind" (Matt. 22:37 NASB), cannot be experientially carried out in the lives of those who have not yet been evangelized. When Jesus gave His Great Commission to "go and make disciples of all nations," the ultimate purpose of that commandment was to help people come to the place where they could fulfill their highest human privilege; that is, to personally know and love God.

One unforgettably beautiful March afternoon, Ruth and the children accompanied me to the summit of the Sandia Mountains of Albuquerque. Suspended high in a gondola looking out over thousands of acres of desert, granite boulders, and pine trees, we watched the rainbow colors of the sun dance on the landscape below. The only visible life was a small squirrel playing on a rock. I was dazzled by the enormous beauty of nature that took on a spiritual quality when observed from the heights of the quiet Swiss-built gondola.

Suddenly, a solitary thought crystallized in my mind. I lifted my young daughters so they could enjoy the view and then asked them a question, "Girls, in all the beauty that you can see, is there anything that has the ability to love God?" My seven-year-old was the first to speak, "The mountains can't love God. The trees can't love God, and neither can the little squirrel." Then with the obvious joy of a dawning understanding, Heidi, age 10, turned to me thoughtfully saying, "Daddy, is that why we're special?" It was a moment of truth for all of us.

Loving God is man's unique privilege; that's why we are special. He put us in the center of His picture and made all the universe around us the frame. We are the apple of His eye! Our ability to love Him is a sacred gift carefully reserved for His highest creation.

Water, wind, soil, and our little animal friends were all made for our benefit, but we alone were made for God. We are loved with an everlasting love, and we have been given the ability to respond to the One who created us. That is what the first commandment is all about. To miss the privilege of loving God for any reason forfeits the true meaning of life.

Our witness about Christ is *good news* because He opened the door for true repentance and love for God from men and women around the world! The objective of evangelism is not so much to keep people from hell as it is to relate them to their loving Father in heaven. "For God did not send the Son into the world to judge the world, but that the world should be saved through Him" (John 3:17 NASB). The Father's desire is that all people might come to know Him and to love Him with the totality of all that they are.

It is with this concern in mind that John gives us this clear definitive word: "For God so loved the world that He gave His only begotten Son, that whoever believes in Him should not perish, but have eternal life" (John 3:16 NASB). This means that the message of evangelism is intended to bring men and women to the assurance that when they die, they will not have to meet God as their Judge but rather as their loving Father.

The heart of evangelism is introducing a man to his Creator. The Bible teaches that we cannot know the living God as our Father until we repent of our sins and are forgiven through faith in Jesus Christ. Only through the experience of conversion can we become His children and have the right to call Him "Father." This is not privilege reserved only for adults. Once Jesus chided His disciples for not allowing children to come and see Him. He said, "Let the little children come to me, and do not hinder them, for the kingdom of God belongs to such as these. I tell you the truth, anyone who will not receive the kingdom of God like a little child will never enter it" (Mark 10:14-15). Christ indicated that if we do not have the kind of faith they have, we will never experience the kingdom of God.

Spontaneous Love

When you observe the natural love children have for their parents, it's the most spontaneous kind of love imaginable. I have joyfully experienced this myself when my two daughters have unexpectedly thrown their little arms around me and given me a sweet kiss. In the same way, God is pleased when His children respond to Him in spontaneous affection. He loves each one of us with an everlasting love and desires our love in return.

This is vividly illustrated throughout the Old Testament in His special relationship with the nation of Israel. He loved His people dearly and delighted in teaching them faithfulness. Over and over again He demonstrated His mercy and forgiveness when they spurned His divine love (Neh. 9:18-21).

Jesus' last allegorical teaching to His disciples was on this highly significant theme. He was on His way to the garden called Gethsemane after the upper room discourse when He said, "You did not choose me, but I chose you to go and bear fruit—fruit that will last" (John 15:16 NIV). This all-important fruit that Christ talked about in the life of His disciples was love. He admonished them saying, "By this is My Father glorified, that you bear much fruit, and so prove to be My disciples . . . abide in My love" (John 15:8, 9c NASB).

When people mistakenly interpret Jesus' use of the term "fruit" to simply mean soulwinning, they fail to realize the amazing teaching of this portion of Scripture. In His parting evening of instruction, the Lord constantly repeated two terms, "fruit" and "love." What Jesus was saying was that He had *chosen* and *ordained* His followers (KJV) to go forth and produce love for God in others. The quality of love produced in those who respond to our witness will last, and that is the essential ingredient that we may expect in their lives. The true believer will have an enduring love for God that will last eternally! Unless we understand that "fruit" means "love" in this passage, we may overlook the most distinctive marks of a disciple: his love for God and his love for fellow believers.

We must always impress on the hearts of our Timothys that evangelism is not a duty, but a natural response of love for God flowing out of our lives to others. Evangelism is not a burden. It is pictured in the Bible as a flowing stream or by beautiful rivers (Gen. 2:10-14) and the river of the water of life (Rev. 22:1). Jesus once said, "Whoever believes in me, as the Scripture has said, streams of living water will flow from within him" (John 7:38). This means that a witness is privileged to be a channel of the life-giving Spirit of God.

Everywhere we go as Christian witnesses there should be new life, new faith, and people being born into the kingdom of God. This overflowing lifestyle was particularly evident in the ministry of the apostle Paul. In every city he saw people being changed by his winsome convicting witness (Acts 13:49).

Every believer can have this same experience. The Christian who is committed to a lifestyle of evangelism and who is sensitive to the enabling power of the Holy Spirit will bear lasting fruit. That unique fruit will be love for God from individuals who have responded to the gospel.

Developing Spiritual Vision

What do you want your Timothy to learn about evangelism during your early meetings together? Remember that biblical truths are seldom impressed on a person's heart in one simple Bible study or discussion. Lessons in evangelism have to be demonstrated over and over again, for vision is not so much taught as it is caught.

Jesus practiced this in His own training ministry with His disciples. Seldom do we find Him emphasizing anything only once. Frequently He would portray a truth in parable, and then demonstrate its meaning in a real-life situation.

Emulating the example of Jesus, we must motivate our Timothys by making sure that they have an early awareness that the harvest is ripe! The need calls for an urgent response. Jesus said, "The harvest *is* plentiful, but the workers are few. Ask the Lord of the harvest, therefore, to send out workers into his harvest field" (Luke 10:2). Here Jesus illustrates the vision of evangelism and emphasizes the major hindrance in fulfilling the Great Commission.

Archaeologists and historians tell us that there may have been as many as 750,000 to 1,000,000 people in the region of Galilee at the time of Christ. They had clustered in that fertile area because of its close proximity to the Sea of Galilee, which was their major source of fresh water and food.

Against this background, Jesus was sending seventy of His disciples out two by two, telling them that the spiritual harvest was plentiful. There was absolutely no lack of potential in the response that they could expect. The only difficulty was in the number of trained workers who were available to God. Not only were the seventy sent to reap this enormous harvest but also to pray that God would give them co-workers to labor by their side. They were to desire and to expect that God would raise up fellow workers in answer to their prayers.

Today, as disciples, we are still to pray, "O God, bring Hans, bring Mary, bring Dr. Kim down the street, bring Ingrid, and send them to join us in the joy of the harvest."

In the large denomination of which I am a member, we have painfully discovered that even in our best years, fewer than five percent of our laity and clergy combined have led anyone to a saving knowledge of Jesus Christ. This serious spiritual condition need not exist. However, this alarming statistic accurately reflects the contemporary fact that Christendom at large is suffering from an impaired vision. We have lost sight of the spiritual hunger and openness to the gospel on the part of millions of people in every nation.

Your Timothy is vitally important to the Great Commission because each Christian has been endued by God to bear an empowered witness (Acts 1:8). The last thing God wants is to see His children in a condition of blindness, weakness, or spiritual ignorance. We already have an army of people who are gazing longingly at the less than five percent who are out in the fields effectively reaping the harvest. Many of these bystanders are praying for the workers, appreciating the work being done and even helping pay their wages, *but they do not know the joy of personally participating in the harvest themselves.* Your Timothy will invest a lifetime in Christian service either reaping the harvest or merely watching his fellow workers. The effectiveness of your ministry will play a major role in determining the degree of his participation in evangelism.

Jesus knew that the worldwide need for evangelism would be a challenge for His followers in His day, and that hasn't changed across the centuries. The persistent problem the church has faced is not an unresponsive world but the dearth of people equipped to participate in the harvest.

Participants in Evangelism

Why this emphasis on apprenticing a Timothy? Why is disciplemaking returning to the forefront in the thinking of the church today? Because it is disciples who become lifelong participants in the harvest of God's kingdom.

In the western world people have traditionally looked to the evangelist or paid staff member to carry out the ministry of evangelism.

However, the message of the modern discipleship movement is that every layman, every pastor, every man and woman, boy and girl, is to be motivated with the vision of evangelism and be fully equipped to participate in the harvest.

The serious need of this understanding was vividly brought to my attention through the recent experience of a close friend. He was pastoring a large church, and as he shared with his people the New Testament vision of winning their city for Christ, he encountered the unexpected and strong resistance of the church board. They told him that he was entirely too evangelistic and that his primary calling was to look after them and meet their spiritual needs.

Tragically, they failed to comprehend the fact that his repeated efforts to equip them for personal witness was their spiritual need! Their concept of the role of a pastor was introverted and spiritually immature. They wanted hospital visits, devotional talks, weddings and funerals, but had no burning desire to be equipped for the harvest. God eventually moved their pastor to better soil!

We all need encouragement; we need the prayers of one another so that we can effectively reap in our localities. Spiritual reaping is to be the collective effort of the whole Christian community. We need Baptists and Methodists and Presbyterians and Independents and all other Christians. We need to pray that God will inspire and raise up His people to participate in every nation (Matt. 24:14).

I asked a Christian businessman friend of mine, "Gene, are people getting harder or easier to win to Christ?"

He answered, "Billie, in my life, I've never seen a time when it's been as easy to win people to Christ as it is today. They're simply waiting for someone to share the Lord with them. All we have to do is talk to them forthrightly and not beat around the bush."

Telling fellow church members to witness is not enough. Challenging them with life's greatest opportunity by taking them *with you* and allowing them to observe and personally experience evangelism can change their future. This simple apprenticing process can within our generation change the worldwide impact of evangelism through the church.

Training for Evangelism

How do you create a conscious awareness of the lostness of man? Remember, this is a prerequisite for effective instruction in the life of your Timothy. You can begin by sharing Luke 10:2 and dramatizing its meaning with a real-life application project. Take him out to your car and say, "I don't want you to talk to me for the next hour. Simply meditate on what you're going to see, and let me show you the harvest."

Then drive him slowly up and down the streets of his own city. Show him the nicest homes; take him to the slums; show him the business district; cover the city. Show him the harvest! Make him conscious that God has given him *this* mission field. He does not live in this city by accident, but God in His sovereignty saved him and placed him there. Spiritually this city belongs to him: he is to help win it to Christ and hold it until the Lord comes again.

If all new Christians were given the benefit of this kind of tour, they would have their eyes opened, and the Holy Spirit would break their hearts. They would begin to see the city as God sees it. Before long they would grow to understand the spirit of Jesus when He cried, "O Jerusalem, Jerusalem . . . how often I have longed to gather your children together, as a hen gathers her chicks under her wings, but you were not willing" (Matt. 23:37).

Every Christian needs to have his or her heart broken over the lost condition of people. Most have never seen the harvest with spiritual eyes or been led to view their personal ministry in these terms.

When you return home from taking your Timothy on this drive, sit down and say, "Do you know what God's plan is for reaching this city? Who will participate in reaping this wonderful harvest?" Then turn to the Scriptures and read together: "For it is by grace you have been saved, through faith—and this is not from yourselves, it is the gift of God—not by works, so that no one can boast. For we are God's workmanship, created in Christ Jesus to do good works, which God prepared in advance for us to do" (Eph. 2:8-10). Then say to him:

"Now John, by the grace of God, you have been saved and you have been reborn spiritually through faith in Jesus Christ for the specific purpose of *doing good works.*"

Then explain to him that in the Bible doing good works means having a personal ministry (Rev. 14:13). A good work is not merely a humanitarian effort, but is a God-inspired, God-empowered, and God-led life of spiritual service. Then continue:

"John, you were created and formed for a ministry that God has prepared for you. You have no idea how important you are to God. He's got a whole section of the harvest with your name on it."

It is essential that the new convert who is now your Timothy realize that he is unique and special. He is to harvest love for God, for that is what evangelism is all about. He is to have a ministry that will ultimately produce more fruit—love for God—and that fruit will remain for all eternity.

It is exciting to challenge a new Christian with this vision, because he can see that he is about to do something that will last forever. To fulfill his life's mission, he has no choice but to involve himself in the harvest.

Robert Coleman has said that if your heart is ever to be gripped with a sense of destiny, you have to see the value of your part in the strategy of God for this world. As long as you are unaware of your part in God's strategy, anything you do will seem insignificant and mundane. But when you realize that every single one of us as Christians has a vital part in the plan of God, then you will have the incentive to commit yourself to being and doing what God wants in your life.

Conclude this session with your Timothy with something like this:

"John, as your Paul, it will be my privilege to help you find *your* ministry. That's going to be my major responsibility. My desire is to guide you to become equipped for that ministry and help you understand God's will so you can have an abundant and useful life that pleases Him. Make it your constant objective to not miss the purpose for which you have been created."

If you start out like this with a new Timothy, then as he grows in his quiet time, Scripture memory, Bible study, character development, and other spiritual disciplines, he will naturally see their relationship to evangelism. With this balanced perspective, Satan will find it difficult to produce a dichotomy between spritual growth and evangelism.

The *motivation* for evangelism is to produce eternal love for God and to fulfill the first and greatest commandment (Deut. 6:5). The *vision* of evangelism is to see the harvest and become a worker in it, praying for others to join you (Luke 10:2). The *participants* in evangelism are all Christian, for all have been created in Christ Jesus to do those things that please Him (Eph. 2:10).

Whenever you have led a person to love God, then you have produced fruit that will bring glory to Him. Every time you lead someone to Christ and he starts loving God, you have produced the first natural fruit of the Spirit.

The Issue Is Love

While on a vacation in Michigan, I met a young man named Frank at a service station. I noticed on the front of his T-shirt a picture of a man drinking. The caption read: "Liquor isn't hard; drinking is the easiest thing I do."

I couldn't help but think that this man was saying he loved liquor. So I said to him, "You know, it takes a lot of courage to do what you're doing."

He was startled and asked, "How's that?"

I replied, "I've been watching you fill up my car, and I've been trying to think what I love enough, respect enough, and care enough about that I'd be willing to advertise for it twenty-four hours a day, putting it on my body and wearing it for all the world to see. It takes a lot of courage for you to advertise liquor the way you do and express your deep love for it."

He looked completely shell-shocked. He had never thought through what the message of his shirt was really saying. He said, "Oh, you mean this T-shirt?"

"I've been thinking about what I would put on my clothes, if I were going to give free advertising for something. I guess I would have to use a favorite verse of Scripture."

"You would?"

"Yes, I think I would choose Paul's statement 'For to me, to live is Christ and to die is gain' (Phil. 1:21). I believe that sums up everything that I really believe to be important in life."

He looked surprised. My next question seemed natural: "Let me ask you something. Do you think there will be drinking parties in heaven?"

"No, sir," he replied (he was about 19).

"Well, then, the thing you really love won't be in heaven, will it?"

"I guess it won't."

"Do you think the other things you like will be in heaven?"

"No, I don't guess they will."

"I don't think you'd enjoy heaven very much then."

"I've never really thought about that."

I said, "Frank, are you planning on going there?"

"Yes, sir," he replied, "I'd like to go there."

"Well, I would like to ask you why. I mean, I can't see how you would enjoy being some place where all you would do is praise and love God, if that isn't what you enjoy now."

The further we went in our conversation, the more he came under conviction. I became excited as I began to understand something that I'd never seen so clearly before.

I said, "Frank, did you know that the Bible tells us that in heaven we will praise God, magnify God, sing to God, worship God, and fellowship with God? When we get right down to it, that's basically what we do in church down here on earth. We praise Him and talk about Him; we talk to Him in prayer and fellowship with Him and with each other. You know, if you don't enjoy those things with God's people down here, heaven would be a real disappointment. Imagine being in heaven for all eternity."

It became clear that for Frank to be happy in eternity, one of two things would have to occur; either the wonder of heaven would have to be completely changed, or Frank would have to be completely changed by asking for God's help.

The conversation continued, "I think that hell may really be the best place for you. You might just as well accept the fact that you're getting plenty of practice for an eternity without God. Jesus Christ talked a great deal about hell and said that people go there only by their own choice. Sin is always a deliberate act of the will."

After a few more minutes of discussion, he saw the issue clearly. I briefly shared with him the testimony of a young man who made the decision to give his heart to Christ, and by the end of that illustration, Frank wanted to know how to talk to God about changing his own eternal destiny.

Our conversation began with analyzing just what it was that Frank loved. A person will tell you about what he loves in many different ways; the object of Frank's love was made clear by the advertisement on his T-shirt.

Until a person understands where he is headed, he has no desire to change his direction. I have found that most lost people subconsciously want to go to heaven, but have little or no understanding about why they would like to go there. Their heaven is often one invented in their own imagination which has little or no resemblance to the heaven portrayed in God's Word.

The issue in salvation is love. Everyone loves something. The point of evangelism is to redirect that love toward God through faith in His Son, the Savior Jesus Christ.

2

Evangelism Flows Out of a Godly Life

One of the most important lessons you will ever learn and teach your Timothy is that evangelism flows out of a godly life. You will win no more people and exert no more influence for the Savior than the quality of your life allows.

If you have had a genuine conversion experience and even know how to share it, but fail to develop a godly character that is conformed to the image of Christ, you will be barren and ineffective in personal evangelism. To say it plainly, you cannot expect to witness successfully while being content with a spiritually mediocre life.

The Cleansing Power of the Word of God

What an encouragement it must have been for the early disciples when they heard Jesus say, "You are already clean because of the word I have spoken to you" (John 15:3). Just as a farmer prunes back his trees to produce a better yield, Jesus carefully groomed His apostles for effective service. Above all else, their lives had to be pure.

At the start of His own ministry, Jesus revealed the secret of how to live a pure and victorious life. He told the tempter, "It is written: 'Man does not live on bread alone, but on every word that comes from the mouth of God' " (Matt. 4:4, quoted from Deut. 8:3). *It is daily intake and yieldedness to God's Word* that determines how He can use you. The Scriptures are our

Source of spiritual strength. They build a Christian character that meets the lifelong prerequisite for effective evangelism.

I seldom find a believer who does not desire to be used by God. But it is also true that I seldom meet a believer who understands the cost of being used by God.

Learning to live in *obedience* to God's will as revealed through His Word is the key to experiencing an abundant personal ministry. We know this because obedience was the preoccupation of Jesus during His earthly life. Paul wrote the church at Philippi: "Your attitude should be the same as that of Christ Jesus, Who . . . made himself nothing, taking the very nature of a servant, being made in human likeness. And being found in appearance as a man, he humbled himself and became obedient to death—even death on a cross!" (Phil. 2:5-8).

To be fully effective in evangelism, you and your Timothy must emulate Jesus in His willingness to please the Father. Obedience to His leadership must become your continual and highest goal in life. This begins slowly and grows through wholehearted allegiance to God's Word.

A Winsome Witness

Evangelism flows out of a well-balanced life. Your friendliness will allow people to identify with you in a natural way. People are attracted to those who know how to laugh, sing, engage in athletics, and enjoy just being *real*. This special quality of reality comes only from God, who is the source of our witness. Jesus spoke of that source, "The words I say to you are not just my own. Rather, it is the Father, living in me, who is doing his work" (John 14:10).

The Father is the One who desires to do the work of witness through us. The key to making that witness natural is simply praying, "Lord, is this You prompting my concern? If it is, I am eager for You to speak. Please don't let me get in Your way. Just let me relax in faith as You do it through me."

God wills to work through us and through our Timothys. Though in ourselves we cannot lead anyone to Christ, the Holy Spirit is faithful to do it. He uses us as His instruments of witness out of the overflow of His new life within us. When we are yielded, evangelism is totally natural in the lives of believers because of the indwelling presence of the Spirit of God. "For it is God who is at work in you, both to will and to work for His good pleasure" (Phil. 2:13 NASB).

Purity in Our Character Is a Choice

I have never known a man or woman who has been significantly used by God, who has come to that place without gaining victory in the area of personal purity. Temptation is no respecter of persons, so everyone who works in the kingdom of God is going to be tempted in many ways during his life. Satan wants to destroy the testimony of Christians, so he tries to sully them and tempt them to compromise with sin. His objective is to produce the continual presence of guilt in our lives. However, Christ has given us His full and effective victory in this regard. The Scripture promises, "If we confess our sins, He is faithful and righteous to forgive us our sins and to cleanse us from all unrighteousness" (1 John 1:9 NASB).

Because temptations are going to come, you and your Timothy need to understand that your purity of thought and your singleness of purpose are of supreme importance to God. Your purity is not determined for you. It requires your personal *choice*. Ponder what the apostle Paul wrote to Timothy: "Now in a large house there are not only gold and silver vessels, but also vessels of wood and of earthenware, and some to honor and some to dishonor. Therefore, *if* a man *cleanses himself* from these things, he will be a vessel for honor, sanctified, useful to the Master, prepared for every good work" (2 Tim. 2:20-21 NASB).

In this passage Paul explains to Timothy that there are four levels of ministry that we can experience as believers. We can choose to be vessels of gold, silver, wood, or clay. Some of these articles are for higher purposes than others. You would not use a gold pot for cooking spaghetti. Your gold and silver vessels are your finest possessions. They are designed for beauty. Other articles in your home, however, are not as valuable and are designed for what Paul calls "dishonorable" purposes. These are made of wood and clay.

The key to a successful ministry is found in the phrase, "if a man cleanses himself." In context it speaks of abstaining from godless conversation (v. 16), wickedness (v. 19), lustful desires (v. 22), and foolish arguments (v. 23). All of these sins are choices having to do with our purity.

"If a man cleanses *himself*!" It does not say that we are to cleanse our wives, children, friends, and fellow believers. Nor does it say that others are to help cleanse me. It does say that I must cleanse *myself*.

If a man cleanses himself from these things, he will be an instrument for honorable purposes in the hands of God. The vessel that will honor God most will be the one that has *chosen* to be clean. He will be like gold or silver.

Tragically, many Christians settle for being pottery; they never bear an effective testimony, never really learn the Word of God or choose a life of uncompromising moral and ethical standards. Because of failure to aspire to be vessels of gold, they fail to lead others to Christ and make little impact on their family and friends.

The word "if" implies that each of us has this God-given choice. No one has been predestined to be impure; it is not foreordained that a Christian be mediocre or half-hearted; it is not determined that he be undisciplined, unloving, or unjoyful. In fact, the opposite is true. Jesus Christ came to give us life and to give it to us abundantly (see John 10:10). His plan for us is that we have a progressively upward journey with Him.

Humility Is Also a Personal Choice

I was visiting with Grady Wilson, my earliest Paul, on one occasion and asked him, "Grady, how do you and Billy Graham handle pride? How do you keep yourselves spiritually clean in that area?"

He answered, "We deal with it the way Peter instructed us. He said, 'Humble yourselves, therefore, under God's mighty hand' (1 Peter 5:6). Humility is a personal daily choice. Don't ask God to humble you. Don't ask your wife to humble you. Don't ask your Christian friends to humble you. Humble yourself."

Grady continued, "Billie, the first time you ever pray for God to humble you, you will be in *big* trouble! God knows how to humble people. If you read the Old Testament, you will find several kings He humbled. You wouldn't want to go through what they did."

God once put a mighty ruler named Nebuchadnezzar out in the pasture lands to eat grass like a common animal because it took that to humble him (Dan. 4:31-36). In the end, the king said, "I quit" (Dan. 4:37). Ultimately, in the pursuit of a man's best interests, God can always humble him if he refuses to humble himself.

Paul later taught the same concept in his first letter to Timothy: "Train *yourself* to be godly" (1 Tim. 4:7). In his second letter he tells Timothy to cleanse *himself*. The theme is clear: Humble yourself. Train yourself. Cleanse yourself. Don't sit around and say, "God, when You finally make me humble and clean, then I will serve You."

It is far better for you to use your own volition to humble and cleanse yourself. Perhaps the highest privilege of being made in the image of God is your ability to choose your own character. You were forgiven at Calvary and now you have the God-given ability to decide to walk in purity on a daily, hourly basis.

Plan Ahead for Victory

To have a clean mind and a lifestyle of purity, you need to plan ahead to avoid temptation. You will have to discipline yourself carefully in what you read, in the entertainment in which you participate, and in the choice of your companions. "Leave the presence of a fool, or you will not discern words of knowledge" (Prov. 14:7 NASB).

If you have trouble with an unclean mind, you cannot blame someone else for your condition. If you continue in sin, you are simply not facing your problem head on. "Finally, brethren, whatever is true, whatever is honorable, whatever is right, whatever is pure, whatever is lovely, whatever is of good repute, if there is any excellence and if anything worthy of praise, let your mind dwell on these things" (Phil. 4:8).

While preaching in Germany, I met a young man who had been spending all his time drinking and dancing at bars. The night he was saved, he asked me how to avoid sin in the future. He came from a handsome eastern race noted for their dark olive complexions. As we talked, he said, "Billie, I need some help because I have more spiritual problems than the average person. I have a theory. The darker a person's complexion, the more vulnerable he is to temptation."

I could not help but chuckle. His theory was not only humorous but unbiblical. All men, according to the Scriptures, are tempted without distinction as to race, complexion, or nationality. Paul said very clearly, "No temptation has seized you except what is common to man. And God is faithful; he will not let you be tempted beyond what you can bear. But when you are tempted, he will also provide a way out so that you can stand up under it" (1 Cor. 10:13).

I then shared with my new Christian friend a favorite illustration from the folklore of the American Indian.

A young brave came to a wise old chief and said, "Chief, I have small twin dogs. One of them is brown, the other speckled." He continued, "I am going to let these two small dogs fight. Can you tell me which one will win the fight?"

The old Indian smiled and answered, "The one that you feed the most."

That sage answer did not come from the Bible, but its practical application agrees with the Scriptures. As a Christian, you have two natures that are in conflict with one another. In daily experience it is a guaranteed result that the one you feed is the one that will win. You may be a dedicated, born-again believer and even be called to a special form of ministry, but it is certain that the nature you feed—the old nature or the new nature—is the one that will become the stronger and will predominate.

In order to cleanse yourself daily, you will have to starve your old nature and feed your new nature with the Word of God, spiritual praise, and fellowship with growing believers. The key is feeding on the Word of God daily through your quiet time and obeying the Scriptures. This will develop gold and silver character qualities in your life.

There is only one kind of instrument that a skilled surgeon cannot use. He can use one that is bent, crooked, old, or new, but he cannot use a *dirty* instrument, no matter how perfect and beautiful it may be otherwise.

The same is true in the Christian life. The only kind of person God cannot and will not use is one who has a dirty life. He can use us in spite of our ignorance; He can use us with our personality defects and our idiosyncracies. But He will never use a life characterized by impurity until it is cleansed.

If you desire to be used of God in multiplication evangelism, if you decide to be a godly man or woman, if you choose to be pure, if you plan to succeed in your ministry, and if you trust Him to accomplish it through you, *then it is a foregone conclusion that you will have victory.* "The one who calls you is faithful and he will do it" (1 Thess. 5:24).

The Importance of the Word of God

It is impossible to conceive of a Christian having a strong evangelistic or training ministry without having a good grip on the Word of God. Every believer, particularly a trainer of Timothys, must develop a good working knowledge of the Bible.

This does not come easily or without opposition from Satan. He will do anything and everything to divert us from the Word of God. It takes great diligence to be in the Scriptures on a daily basis.

In order to have a productive evangelistic ministry, your daily walk needs to be consistent in the areas of quiet time, Bible reading, Bible study, and Scripture memory. "So then, just as you received Christ Jesus as Lord, continue to live in him, rooted and built up in him, strengthened in the faith as you were taught, and overflowing with thankfulness" (Col. 2:6).

Paul complimented the church in Berea for their commitment to the Word of God: "Now the Bereans were of more noble character than the Thessalonians, for they received the message with great eagerness and examined the Scriptures *every day* . . . (Acts 17:11). It is consistency that builds useability. Your devotional life is the platform on which your ministry is built. The Scriptures will become an enriching and natural part of your life as you enjoy them daily.

Responsible Speech

Jesus sternly warned His generation that they were accountable for their words. He said, "But I tell you that men will have to give account on the day of judgment for every careless word they have spoken. For by your words you will be acquitted, and by your words you will be condemned" (Matt. 12:36-37). Earlier He had said in the Sermon on the Mount, "Simply let your 'Yes' be 'Yes', and your 'No' 'No' " (Matt. 5:37).

The Bible teaches that we are to be consistent in what we are and in what we say. Let your "yes" mean something. Be the kind of person who will be listened to when you speak. Do not exaggerate the truth. Let your "no" be a "no" of conviction and integrity, not an idle word that has no substance.

This has serious implications in evangelism. When the time comes to share the plan of salvation with someone, you need authority in your testimony or witness that is backed up by your life. One close friend says it this way, "To be effective, a Christian's walk and talk must be the same."

While teaching as a guest professor at Columbia Bible College in Columbia, South Carolina, I exercised each day in the gym. After each workout, I would go to a nearby restaurant and order a health shake—a milkshake with some good fruit and wheat germ in it. At the end of the three-weeks' term, I told the waitress how much I had appreciated her service and graciousness and that I would not be back.

"Oh," she said, "you are not from South Carolina?"

"No," I replied, "I'm from Texas and will be going home at the end of this week."

"Well, what brought you to South Carolina?"

I had been praying for an opportunity to witness to her for two weeks, but the door had never seemed to open until now. I told Rhonda that I had been teaching the Bible at a nearby Christian college.

Seeming surprised that anyone who would teach the Bible would work out in a gym and drink health shakes, she immediately replied, "Well, I guess that is all right as long as you are not a Baptist."

It was somewhat difficult for me to know how to respond. A slight smile crept over my face as I said, "I hate to tell you this, but I am a Baptist."

"Well, I guess that is all right, too, if you are not a Southern Baptist."

"I am really sorry to have to tell you this, but I am a Southern Baptist."

"You sure did ruin my sister!" she retorted.

"What happened to your sister?"

"She was a perfectly normal religious person who went to the military chapel on the base. Everything was fine in our home until my sister had what she called a born-again experience at an evangelistic meeting. It has literally ruined her; she is the most miserable person I know."

"Did she tell you she was miserable?"

Instead of answering my question, she continued, "I'll tell you how bad it is. She doesn't cuss anymore; she doesn't drink; she doesn't smoke; she won't even roller skate."

"Rhonda, that last one is carrying it a little too far, but has your sister told you that she is miserable?"

"No. In fact, she actually thinks she is happy! But she must be crazy. Nobody could be happy and live like that."

The feeling Rhonda had about her sister is typical of those who do not understand what happens in the life of a person who commits himself or herself to Jesus Christ. Such attitudes are quickly dispelled as the Holy Spirit uses your testimony and the Scriptures to enlighten their understanding. "I have chosen the faithful way; I have placed Thine ordinances before me" (Ps. 119:30 NASB).

I briefly shared with Rhonda the biblical story of Mary and Martha, explaining that her sister, like Mary, had simply chosen the better alternative in life. After a few moments of conversation, Rhonda began to cry. Her obvious deep need gave me the opportunity to share the plan of salvation. She sat down at the counter while I drew the Bridge Illustration[1] on a napkin, and she received Christ as her Savior and Lord that day.

Loving Patience

One of my Pauls is a gracious theologian and evangelist from India, Dr. A. B. Masilamani. When he began preaching as a young man, people would not let him into their homes. Often he would stand in the dusty street preaching and teaching the Bible, while his Hindu audience sat on the porches of their houses listening. As the Holy Spirit began to deal with the people of his city, they began inviting him to come into their front yards. Finally, they invited him to their front steps and even on to the front porches with them.

Many months went by before they honored him by inviting him into their homes. At first the people sat in their chairs while he sat on the floor. Today when Dr. Masilamani visits the homes of these former Hindus who have now come to know Jesus, they have him sit in the chair and they all sit on the floor at his feet as he breaks the Bread of Life for them.

This dear man was willing to wait on God for results while persisting in bearing his witness. Because of his life, I have asked myself many times if I would be willing to stand patiently outside the gates in the dusty street and proclaim the gospel to

---

[1]Section in Book see pp. 69-75.

people in their homes. Would I humble myself and continue to sit on the floor while others sat in comfortable chairs so that I might explain the Good News to them? Would I persist in trying to give these people the most valuable gift in life in spite of their continual rejection? This is the kind of question that you must ask with regard to family members and close friends whom you deeply love but who continually reject the goodness and grace of God. Remember that some who come slowly become the strongest disciples of all.

Whole-Hearted Commitment

Whole-heartedness has been a problem for the people of God across the centuries. A sad epitaph for one of Judah's kings reads, "And he did right in the sight of the LORD, yet not with a whole heart" (2 Chron. 25:2 NASB). Amaziah was twenty-five when he became king in Jerusalem, and he reigned for twenty-nine years, but he lived a half-hearted life.

God forbid that an inscription like that be written over our lives. I do not want to come to the end of my life and have it said, "Billie Hanks was a good old boy. He loved God, but he only served God with half his heart. He did the right things but was constantly wishing that he were doing something else."

Whether you are a pastor, a missionary, or a layman, this tragic epitaph serves as a warning. Amaziah was in the will of God vocationally; he was king and that is what God wanted him to be. He was in the will of God geographically and chronologically; he was king in the right place at the right time. But he was half-hearted in his service to God. No sin, other than impurity, will more greatly hamper the work of evangelism than half-hearted, lukewarm commitment to Christ. "I know your deeds, that you are neither cold nor hot; I would that you were cold or hot. So because you are lukewarm, and neither hot nor cold, I will spit you out of My mouth" (Rev. 3:15-16 NASB).

God desires our whole-hearted enthusiastic commitment to doing His will. If half-heartedness is considered average in the life of your church, then your positive example can be God's way of breathing new life and spiritual vitality into the fellowship. Paul Harvey puts it this way, "To be average is to be the best of the lousy or the lousiest of the best." God does not want you to be an average layman; He does not want you to be an average missionary; He does not want you to be an average Christian. He wants you to be a man or woman of God who is totally sold out to Him—and that's not average!

Your witness will abound as the wellspring of your relationship with God overflows from your life. James said, "Draw near to God and He will draw near to you" (James 4:8 NASB). That promise remains eternally true. If you have never had the privilege of leading someone to Christ, drink deeply from the living waters of His Word in your daily quiet time. Make up your mind right now to pray and then take the necessary practical steps to develop a godly character. Hide the six major verses on the plan to salvation in your heart (see chap. 5), so you will be able to share them. Decide to be a positive witness! Determine not to live an average life.

3

Sharing a Word of Truth

Over the years I have found it helpful to categorize witnessing opportunities three ways. Just as a hammer, chisel, and saw have three different functions related to carpentry, so there are three effective methods of witness related to evangelism. These three approaches are:

1. Sharing a word of truth: briefly imparting a single truth about God (discussed in this chapter).

2. Sharing a testimony: expressing the difference Christ has made in your life (chap. 4).

3. Sharing the plan of salvation: explaining from Scripture how to come to know Christ personally (chap. 5).

Sharing a Word of Truth

Sharing *a* word of truth (not *the* entire message of the gospel) means giving a casual, brief witness. It may be called a "wayside witness." It is usually terse, uncomplicated, and something any Christian can do.

When my Paul first began to disciple me in personal evangelism, he taught me to share the plan of salvation (category 3). This presentation usually takes twelve to fifteen minutes. However, sometimes there is not that much time available.

At first I went around looking for people who had fifteen minutes to listen. If I couldn't find anyone with this much time, I assumed I wasn't supposed to witness.

When you are eager to share, it is frustrating not to be able to do it. So I went to my Paul and said, "You know, it's wonderful that I've been able to lead some people to Christ, but there are dozens of people I meet every day to whom I could witness if I only knew how to do it in a shorter length of time."

He said, "Well, Billie, can't you just share a word of truth about Jesus Christ?"

"What do you mean?"

"Any true word about God is a witness," he replied. "You can just share a brief portion of the gospel. It doesn't have to be the entire plan of salvation."

This was a great relief to me because I had thought the only way to help people was to go from A to Z. I didn't realize that I could effectively witness in a less structured, less formal manner.

The next week Ruth and I were driving to Uvalde, Texas. I was a little frustrated because we were running tight on time.

When we pulled into a service station, the young attendant grunted as he removed the gasoline cap and filled the tank. I soon discovered he had zero personality. I gave him my credit card and went inside to sign the ticket. As I was walking back out to the car, the Holy Spirit began to tug at my heart.

"Billie, I want you to share a word of truth with that man."

I hoped that I was talking to myself.

Reaching the car I said, "Ruth, I want you to pray for me. I believe the Lord wants me to witness to the station attendant."

She responded, "Honey, you don't have fifteen minutes to spare." (She had learned the same method of witnessing I had.)

"Ruth," I replied, "I'm going to try it a new way. Just pray for me."

So I walked back into the station and looked at the young man. He was a big, strapping fellow, about eighteen or nineteen years old, and looked like half the football team of that little town. Having mustered up my courage, I prayed, "Lord, how do You want me to do this?"

I said, "Sir!"

He looked at me without saying a word.

"I want to tell you something. I have a message for you.

God loves you very much, and has sent His Son, Jesus Christ, to die for you on the cross. He's been waiting for you to ask His Son into your heart so He can forgive your sins. He'd like to give you a wonderful life, but He won't force His way in. You'll have to pray and ask Him to come into your heart. The next step is yours. That's the message I'm supposed to deliver to you."

The young man never said a word. He stood there completely speechless. As he looked at me with a thoughtful expression on his face, I slowly walked back to the car. Out of curiosity I turned around and looked through the window. He was still gazing at the wall where I'd been standing.

I drove off with real joy in my heart because I knew I had done what the Lord wanted me to do. It wasn't the right time to open the Bible and show him all the verses, then pray with him. I was just supposed to share a word of truth. For the first time I was conscious of the Holy Spirit's empowering work in a three-minute witness with a stranger.

The Example of Andrew

A word of truth is simply saying what you can about the Lord in a few brief words. Note Andrew's immediate desire after he met Jesus. "The first thing Andrew did was to find his brother Simon and tell him, 'We have found the Messiah' (that is, the Christ)" (John 1:41). The author of this Gospel added the interpretation, but the words actually spoken by Andrew were these: "We have found the Messiah!"

These five words were probably the first witness that Andrew shared with anyone. He had heard John the Baptist bear witness that Jesus was the Lamb of God. This occurred the day after the unforgettable experience when Andrew heard the voice of God saying, "This is my Son, whom I love; with him I am well pleased" (Matt. 3:17), and watched the Holy Spirit descend like a dove as John baptized Jesus.

Andrew was convinced that the Messiah had come, and his witness was very simple. It was a word of truth: "We have found the Messiah!" Now why didn't he talk about the cross?

Why didn't he mention the death, burial, and resurrection of Jesus? Why didn't he introduce the miracles and all the other components of the gospel?

Because none of those things had yet happened. But he did say all that he knew and all that he could, for when a Jewish person says those five words, "We have found the Messiah," he has said it all.

Did his witness bear fruit?

Yes! Peter understood exactly what his brother said, and ultimately became one of the greatest Christians of all time. But it all started with five simple words.

Flexibility of Vocabulary

Another important factor in sharing a word of truth has to do with vocabulary. To the best of your ability, try to use a vocabulary that fits the situation, for not everyone uses the same terminology.

On one memorable occasion when I was going out to dinner in Fort Worth, I stopped at a service station for some gas. A sports car pulled in next to me.

As I got out of my car, I looked down into the window of the sports car at a young man who had the appearance of a hippie. Immediately I wanted to communicate with him in some way that he would understand, but I didn't know many words of his vocabulary.

Feebly I began, "Man, are you into Jesus yet?"

He turned, looked at me, and said, "I've been groovin' on Him lately."

Feeling very inadequate, I breathed a little prayer and said, "*Father, You led me into this, now please help me out!*"

To the hippie I said, "Have you rapped with Him lately?"

"No, man," he replied.

I said, "Let me tell you, He's really heavy. If you'll rap with Him and get to know Him, you'll discover that He's real."

He said, "I dig you."

I was fresh out of vocabulary. I didn't have another word left. So I smiled at him and said, "Friend, Jesus is God and

He's cool. If you rap with Him tonight and really tell Him about your problems and sins, and tell Him that you want to believe in Him and ask Him to come into your heart, He will do it."

And the man said, "Right on. I dig you."

I left him, got back into my car, and sighed a peaceful breath of relief. Even though the words were foreign to me, the special look on the face of that young man and the sincerity in his eyes were the same as those I had seen many times before when the Holy Spirit was dealing with men and women about their need of God. My confidence is that the Holy Spirit will never let him forget that God led someone who knew Christ personally to talk to him.

The Holy Spirit's Leading

God will begin to use you increasingly as you learn to share a word of truth any time and every time He wants you to. As you mature, less and less prompting will be needed to motivate you in the direction of His will.

As a boy I owned an old but well-trained cutting horse. When I began riding Midnight, I discovered that all I had to do was barely touch him with the reins on the side of his neck for him to turn in that direction.

That's the way God wants us to be in terms of witness. Wouldn't you like to be the kind of man or woman whom God could just slightly touch with the leading of His Spirit, and you would immediately turn in the direction of His prompting? Witnessing would occur naturally and according to His will.

When you truly *desire* to be led in witnessing, God will give you a gentle, and soon familiar, touch of His Spirit. You will feel an inner urging to share a word of truth. Sometimes you may not feel impressed to witness, and that can be of God, too. In trying to determine the leadership of the Holy Spirit in witnessing, simply ask, "Father, if this is not of You, take the impression away and leave me with no sense of guilt." But, "If it is of You, Father, and You know that this person is ready and needs to be ministered to, and You want me to witness to him, then please impress it on me harder. Make it so clear that I cannot miss Your leading."

The key to obedience is willingness to do God's will.

God has been faithful over the years to reveal His will when I was willing to do it. I have not always been sensitive to Him, and consequently, there have been some dismal failures.

One day at a car wash, I was waiting behind a lovely elderly woman driving one of the finest Cadillacs I have ever seen. She was elegantly dressed and her hair had a beautiful blue tint just like my grandmother's. She walked with a cane but carried herself with great dignity. The Lord began to prompt me to witness, but I was apprehensive. If she had been a Japanese Sumo wrestler, I couldn't have been more afraid of her. I prayed, "Lord, is this impression to witness really of You? Please take it away if it is not of You, and press it on me harder if it is."

He deepened the impression. However, this elegant woman and I talked about the weather, about the gasoline mileage of her Cadillac, and about everything else except Jesus Christ. I just couldn't get myself to obey the Lord. I hesitated as if she might have hit me with her cane if I mentioned Christ.

At the end of the line, with my car right behind hers, I had a thought. "*I know, I'll get a tract for her out of my glove compartment.*" Though this might normally have been good, in my case it was a copout. I received this fleeting thought from God, "Go ahead and just talk to her about Me."

But I waited too long. My car slowed up after hers was finished, and she left before I could get to the glove compartment. I knew I had failed. I had been disobedient to the Lord. Perhaps I would be the last Christian to have a chance to share Christ with her.

So I jumped in my car and started after her, never quite catching up. Finally as she neared a beautiful residential section, I lost her completely when I was stopped at a traffic light, but I spent half an hour driving around the area looking for her car.

Finally, in frustration, I pulled over to the side of the road, and just broke down and cried. I said, "God, how long does it take for You to get a man to the place where You can trust him? How many years do I have to be a Timothy to a Paul? How many times do I have to re-learn to listen to You? When will You ever be able to trust me? God, please forgive me."

Claiming His forgiveness (1 John 1:9), I asked Him to send a more dedicated and faithful Christian to witness to that woman.

When you train your Timothys in evangelism, don't just tell them all your bright success stories. They may get the impression that you were born with a great big red "S" on your chest and you flew through life like a spiritual Superman. It doesn't happen that way in the Christian life. You grow and you stumble and you fall and you get up—and sometimes you stumble and fall again. You have to choose to be useable on a daily basis. That has been my experience in witnessing. But every time you have a disheartening experience like the one above, God can use it to make you stronger, more sensitive, and more careful to take advantage of the next opportunity.

A New Understanding of Time

Time can be an obstacle in doing God's will if we do not understand that He purchased all the minutes of our life on Calvary. What if Philip had been too busy to obey God on the day when the Ethiopian eunuch was searching for God? (Acts 8:26-39)

Perhaps thousands or even millions of wonderful people are missing Christ today simply because Christians' priorities are out of line with God's will. Those who want to be used by God must be willing to do the unusual. Each year is studded with adventurous memories when you ask God for the daily opportunity of witness. Sometimes He will say no to that prayer. On other occasions, He will tell you to wait. But there will be many times when you will receive a clear and unmistakable yes!

After spending Christmas with the Grady Wilsons in North Carolina, Ruth and I were flying home to Fort Worth. We had a scheduled stop in Atlanta. Now the Atlanta airport is the crossroads of the South, and it is well-known for the long distance to departure gates.

We ate at the Dobbs House restaurant thinking we had plenty of time. But the service was slow, and suddenly it was nearly time to take the long walk to our Texas-bound plane. Just as I began to feel it was time to leave the restaurant, I noticed a soldier sitting by himself at an adjacent table.

Humanly speaking, I did not want to become concerned about him because I didn't have any time, but the Lord impressed him on my heart.

I thought, "*No way, Lord. Please! You know that I don't have the time right now. Surely this is just my own mind thinking I should witness to this man.*" So I prayed, "Lord, take this impression away if it isn't of You," then added, "I'll give him a tract. How would that be?"

Reaching into my brief case, I pulled out a tract. But the Holy Spirit checked me in my spirit, saying, "No, he is not to receive a tract but your witness."

Returning the tract to my brief case, I told Ruth, "Honey, I am supposed to go and talk to that soldier. There is no way that we can catch our plane, but I am sure the Lord wants me to speak to him. You get on the plane and go on to Dallas, and I'll catch the next flight. There's probably a flight every two hours or so."

Ruth replied, "Great!"

Imagine a girl like that! I was so proud to have that kind of wife! She continued, "I'll get on the plane and will be praying that the Lord will bless your witness."

I turned around and looked at the large, tough-looking sergeant. Walking over to his table, I feebly began with, "Sir, are you from Texas?"

"Nope," he answered curtly.

I didn't know where to go from there, but the direct approach is often the best. So I said, "Well, Sir, the truth of the matter is that I have an important message for you and I am supposed to deliver it."

He said, "You are?"

"Yes, Sir. God sent me to speak to you."

"Who?" He was immediately interested. "Pull up a chair and tell me what He wants you to say."

I sat down, looked at him, and said, "He told me to tell you that He loves you, and that He sent His Son to die for you because He really does care about you. He wants to forgive and cleanse you from your sins. He has a place for you in heaven and He wants you to ask Jesus Christ to come into your heart. He wants you to become a real Christian."

Briefly I shared a little bit of my dad's testimony with him because he looked to be in his mid-forties, and my father gave his life to Christ when he was 46.

After a few minutes, I asked, "Would you like to become a Christian?"

"Yep!" he replied.

I thought, "*Hey, this is too easy,*" then said, "Are you sure you want to become a Christian? It really costs to give your life to Christ." It scared me that he had said "OK" so quickly.

He looked at me sternly, and in that deep voice of his said, "Son, I don't say anything that I don't mean." Just like that!

I answered, "Yes, Sir! Do you know how to pray?"

He said, "No, but you can teach me, can't you?"

I liked the way he got right to the point. I said, "Yes, Sir, I can teach you. I will lead you in a prayer but you must pray it from your heart."

Assuming he would pray softly after me, I began, "Lord, I am a sinner."

No sooner had I said that than I heard a loud, deep voice, "LORD, I AM A SINNER!"

I opened my eyes and saw a startled waitress listening to what he was saying, and people at nearby tables looking in our direction. So I spoke more softly, "But I am sorry for my sins."

"BUT I AM SORRY FOR MY SINS," boomed the sergeant.

By the time we were through, some fifteen people around us had inadvertently become aware of his earnest prayer, and that man was gloriously saved. He knew clearly what he was doing. In parting I asked him where he was headed. He said, "Vietnam," and he added, "Thank you, Son. This is what I have wanted all my life. Thank you for showing me how to do it."

How long had this witness taken? Only a few minutes. I was even able to run down the long concourse and catch my plane— on time.

It is a small matter for God to hold a plane, speed up a plane, cancel a flight, or anything else He wants to do. Our part in the divine drama is simply to listen and obey. Once He can trust us in small decisions, He will enlarge the area of our usefulness. The adventure grows and lives are changed as His love flows through our witness by the power of His Spirit. Boredom is incompatible with evangelism, because sharing Christ becomes life's greatest and most exciting experience. Time takes on a new meaning.

Dealing With Problems

1. *Victory over prayerless evangelism.* In the experience of most Christians who desire to witness, there will come the need to distinguish between witnessing out of a sense of obligation and witnessing out of a sense of the Holy Spirit's direct leading. It should be as natural for a Christian to witness as it is for a river to flow. Specific prayer is the key to learning when and how your witness is to be given.

I once heard about a businessman who experienced anxiety when flying on airplanes because he knew that in all likelihood those he sat next to would not be born-again believers. And if his plane should crash, he would be the last person able to lead that man or woman to Christ. The responsibility of that was so enormous that it weighed him down and he became discouraged. At that point in his Christian experience, he had not learned the important role of prayer in determining God's will concerning sharing a witness in every situation.

In witnessing, unwarranted pressure is usually the result of failing to pray and, under God's leadership, appropriate the power of the Holy Spirit. We must not assume prerogatives that belong to Him. It is not our job to decide to whom we are going to witness. It is not even our job to be successful in witnessing. Our responsibility is to consistently remain in the position where we are sensitive to God's leading so that we can be obedient, allowing the Holy Spirit to live and speak through us. It is our daily prayer to be made usable and our desire to share Christ that will make us ready for every God-given opportunity.

Before boarding a certain flight, I specifically prayed about the person who would sit next to me. It is a rewarding practice to pray for divine appointments during each day, God-given opportunities to witness. On this trip the person next to me turned out to be a teenage boy about fifteen or sixteen. I prayed, "Lord, if You want me to witness to this boy, I am eager and ready, but let me know it is Your will by letting it come about naturally."

Taking my Scripture Memory material out, I began to review my memory verses. As I was studying them, the boy looked over to see what I was doing, but I didn't say anything. After a few minutes it just seemed natural to show him one of the verses and say, "Can you explain that verse to me? Tell me what you think it means."

He replied, "Sure, I'll be glad to."

He sat there for a long time studying the verse. Then he said, "OK, Mister, I'm ready," and he explained the meaning of the verse.

I said, "Great; you're right on target. Try this one."

Again he did well, so I gave him a third one. This one was on salvation.

He totally misunderstood its meaning. So I said, "Would you like for me to explain it?"

He replied, "Sure!"

Soon we were discussing the plan of salvation, and before the plane touched down in Denver, he had settled matters with Christ. It was totally natural and ended in peace and spontaneous joy!

2. *Victory over feelings of inadequacy.* This problem is often

the result of a lack of knowledge of God's Word. A friend once talked to a business acquaintance about the fact that he didn't witness. Though successful in business and a leader in his community, he felt like a failure when his first witnessing opportunity ended in confrontation and unanswered questions. He had determined never to witness again until he felt confident in his ability to do it successfully.

Your Timothy may have had a similar experience. If so, assure him that he is not alone in the school of evangelism and that such experiences simply underscore the need for discipline in our lives in the area of Bible study. Point him to specific answers for the excuses he might encounter. The section on "Witnessing Helps" in *The Open Bible* is an excellent place to start learning how to skillfully respond to questions. Knowing the Word of God and how to present it will give him a great deal of security and additional effectiveness (see chap. 4).

3. *Victory over fear.* I have never met a Christian who has not experienced the element of fear in witnessing. Fear diminishes as you gain experience, but it never completely goes away. Fear is just an advanced form of timidity, and it can be used positively in our lives if it reminds us that the Holy Spirit must be the One to do the work. Like a little red light that blinks, the Holy Spirit continually reminds us, "Depend on Me! Depend on Me!" The Lord will give boldness, confidence, and freshness, making witnessing increasingly natural as you apply what you learn experientially.

Fear frequently is the result of failure to appropriate God's resources by faith. That is why Paul wrote to Timothy and said, "For God has not given us the spirit of fear, but of power, and of love, and of a sound mind" (2 Tim. 1:7 KJV). The element that you need to understand in this verse is that God is the One who gives us soundness of mind, peace of heart, and the power to minister. Fear is definitely not from God, but He can use it to remind you of your need for Him. As the psalmist says, "When I am afraid, I will trust in you" (Ps. 56:3).

By faith you and your Timothy must determine to develop spontaneity and overcome fear by carrying out Peter's admonition: "Always be prepared to give an answer to everyone who asks you to give the reason for the hope that you have" (1 Peter 3:15). If you are prepared in your working knowledge of the Scriptures, fear ceases to be a significant problem. Instead, the small amount that remains serves only as a helpful reminder to trust in the Holy Spirit's power rather than your knowledge of the Bible.

4

Sharing Your Testimony

Beyond "sharing a word of truth," the second method of evangelism you need to cultivate and teach your Timothy is that of sharing an effective personal testimony. This means telling the story of how you came to know Christ as your Lord and Savior.

We see this pattern in the life of the apostle Paul. On one occasion he was brought before King Herod Agrippa II, an Idumean king appointed by the Romans over the Jews. "Agrippa said to Paul, 'You have permission to speak for yourself.' So Paul motioned with his hand and began his defense" (Acts 26:1). Paul responded to this opportunity by sharing his own experience with Christ (Acts 26:2-29).

In this instance, Paul didn't merely share a word of truth. He gave a lengthy, detailed personal testimony of what God had done in his life. Often, sharing what God has done in our own lives can communicate more effectively than any other form of witness. This very basic approach to evangelism involves a little more time and frequently requires earning a hearing. Paul earned a hearing with Agrippa by identifying with him. He started out by complimenting him, then told him that because of his background he would be able to understand what Paul was about to say. Soon the king was listening intently.

Different Kinds of Testimonies

We can give many different kinds of testimonies in addition to our conversion experience. Actually, we have a new and different testimony each week of our Christian lives. You may say, "Well, I just have one testimony, because I was saved just once."

This is true concerning salvation, but every time God answers prayer you have a new testimony. Maybe you have been sick and God healed you in answer to the prayers of your family and friends. You may have had financial problems which God solved in a miraculous way. You may have had a difficult interpersonal relationship that God reconciled, or you may even have had major difficulties in your own family that God overcame.

Every one of the above situations gives you a new testimony to share with other people—believers and unbelievers alike. Time after time, God has been faithful, giving you new evidence to share of His grace, mercy, and love. Every day, every week, every month, every year, He demonstrates His adequacy. But the testimony God typically uses most effectively in evangelism has to do with the *event* of your conversion itself.

Your Conversion Testimony

The most important element of a conversion testimony is telling *why* you became a Christian. Why did you decide to become a follower—a disciple—of Jesus Christ? Think of one word that would state as clearly as possible the reason why you became a Christian. Maybe it happened because of conviction . . . fear . . . or loneliness. You could have become aware of the love of God or of the reality of divine *judgment*. You may have made your decision for any of a hundred different reasons.

When you share your testimony with others, tell them what you have experienced and seek to identify honestly with their weaknesses and needs. If you have felt fear, tell them so. If you have been lonely, tell them that. If you have felt alienated from God and became bitter, share that. If you were confused and frustrated and could not understand why there were wars, accidents, famines, and prejudice, say so.

One of the most powerful tools you have to help your fellow men is the ability to aid them in understanding why you as a person of this century decided to give your life to someone who lived 2000 years ago. They must be led to see that your help and inner joy have not come from discovering a new cause or a religious code of ethics, but from a relationship with a vital, living Person, who is eternal. They must understand that you have committed your life to Him on the basis of who He really is and what He did on our behalf.

God allowed us to see His face and sinless character in the person of Jesus Christ so we would desire to know Him personally. This is why He became a man, lived a perfect life before us, and demonstrated His love in the Cross and His power in the Resurrection. Above all, people must be helped to realize the truth that Jesus is God, that they are important to Him, and that His call demands a response.

Why is the issue of *why* being emphasized so much? Because that is what people are really interested in knowing. They do not necessarily want to know *how* you became a Christian. This is not their primary concern. Yet this is what most of us normally tell them. When we are asked to give our testimony, we often say, "I became a Christian at the age of such and such." That tells people *when* we became Christians. Then we go on to tell that it happened in such and such a revival meeting or in a certain location. That is *where* we became Christians.

But the important thing most people want to know is *why* you placed your faith in Him and what He has done for you. In essence, they want to know how He has affected the quality of your life.

What to Emphasize

In sharing your testimony and in teaching your Timothy to share his, there are some occasions when you should not emphasize *when* you were converted. If I were talking to a man in his 40s about Jesus Christ, I would not tell him that I was saved at the age of ten, because he could not identify with my experience. Satan does everything he can to discount your testimony, and telling a forty-year-old man of a childhood conversion helps him do so. That man might then think something like this: "Aha! That boy was educated into Christianity. He didn't have a real experience with God—it was just a psychological or educational process. The boy grew up in a Christian home and went to Sunday school and church, so how can I be sure something really happened to change his life?"

A man who is forty may have become reasonably cynical. He may have seen immaturity, bickering, or hypocrisy in the lives of some church members.

We need to pray that God will help us give our testimonies to different people in the way that will most clearly identify with their need. We must think through what parts of our testimony they most need to hear.

When should you tell people *when* you were converted? If you were sharing your testimony with someone in his 50s, and you came to Jesus when you were forty-five, it would be appropriate to do so. An older adult will be able to identify with the experience of another older adult. He might say something like this to himself, "Well, if you found Christ at this age, and if you have had a change in your life because of faith in Him, maybe I can too."

I have a good friend who was converted at the age of sixty and felt that he had to make up for lost time. In his witnessing experiences for the next twenty years, he generally shared with people who were younger than he. His approach might sound something like this: "Frank, I pray you won't have to wait as long as I did to find the truth. I hope you won't make the same mistake I made. If I had only made this commitment at age forty, what a difference it would have made in my life!"

In sharing our testimonies, there are times when we do say when we were converted and there are other times when we do not. The same is true for *where* we were converted. Sometimes we should mention the location of our conversion; sometimes we should not.

To illustrate this, let's assume that I am a dedicated Christian factory worker about forty-five years of age. I want to share Christ with one of my fellow workers at the factory who is pretty miserable. He is a nice, moral person, but he is lost. He doesn't know Christ, and if he were to die, he would not go to heaven. This has burdened me deeply while we have been working together for over a year.

I happen to know that Jack, my co-worker, likes to fish. Since I am a fisherman, too, I've take the opportunity to ask him to go fishing with me, hoping to be able to share with him what he really needs most in his life—Jesus Christ. Now, imagine that we are fishing, and I will illustrate witnessing *incorrectly* and then *correctly*.

Witnessing Incorrectly

Late on Friday afternoon we arrive at my favorite fishing place and launch the boat. It has been a beautiful afternoon, and the sunset is gorgeous. We are planning to fish into the night.

We aren't out there very long before I say, "Jack, it sure is great to be out here fishing with you. You know, I've been looking forward to getting together so we can talk."

He thought my purpose was fishing, but I have indicated a different purpose before my worm is even wet!

I continue, "Jack, I have been looking forward to asking you if you have ever come to a personal commitment to Jesus Christ. Have you ever given your life to Christ, Jack?"

He answers, "No, I don't suppose I have." I may use all the right religious words, and he may listen out of courtesy.

"Well, Jack, I want to talk to you about that for a few minutes. I would like to tell you that Jesus Christ is wonderful. I gave my life to Him five years ago.

"I visited a little white church building near our home in Louisiana, and an evangelist preached a powerful message. The organ and the piano began to play 'Just As I Am,' the invitation was given to come forward, and Louise and I gave our lives to

Christ. He has been the greatest discovery of my life, Jack, and I would like to challenge you to give your life to Christ as well."

Now all of this may be correct and true, but it may be irrelevant to Jack's need. I haven't told him why I became a Christian—only when, how, and where. Now let's look at a better approach.

Witnessing Correctly

You are out in the boat together, and you notice that the sunset is simply fantastic. Most people like the outdoors and its beauty. You look up from your fishing and say, "Jack, this is just great. It's so peaceful and quiet this evening. Look at that sunset. It's more beautiful than any stained-glass window I've seen."

What is Jack's mental association when you say "stained-glass window"? With church, most likely, for you have helped him into that mindset. Now the difference between this approach and the previous one is that in the first, I took him out of the boat and mentally moved him across the country to Louisiana, where there is a little white church building. I had him waiting for an invitation—a custom with which he probably wasn't familiar. I mentioned a hymn he had never heard and a term, "evangelist," with which he was not familiar.

In the second approach, you're keeping him right in that boat with you. When you comment on the beauty of the sunset reminding you of the colors of a stained-glass window, he agrees.

So you say, "I am always amazed when I realize God can make a world this beautiful." Just about everyone believes in God and thinks the world is a nice place in which to live. You are on safe ground here.

"Yeah," he answers.

Then you may change the subject for a while. When Jesus said, "I will make you fishers of men" (Matt. 4:19), He meant just that. Just as we have to be taught the art of fishing, Christians have to learn the art of witnessing and sharing our testimonies so we can be of help to others. A good fisherman never attempts to set the hook until the fish actually strikes. He has to be patient. When a fish takes the bait, you allow him to run with the line and reel him in slowly.

After having fished awhile, you resume your conversation. You know Jack and his wife have a teenage son with whom they are having serious problems.

"Jack, you sure have a fine-looking son. How is he doing in football?"

"We're proud of him," he replies. "We think he is going to make first string this year."

You reply, "Football was our son's number one love in high school. Those were fun years, but family-wise they were also some of our hardest."

"How's that?"

"We almost lost communication at home. I guess we got too busy in our own worlds. Louise and I even began to feel the strain in our marriage. It got pretty bad for a while."

Jack responds with a note of surprise. "I didn't think that you and your wife ever had any problems."

"Well, we don't right now, but that wasn't true in the past. Even we were surprised how we worked them out."

"Really? What did you do?"

"We tried everything. We read books. We went to a marriage counselor and couldn't find the answers anywhere. So we decided to try something different. We weren't religious people, having only been to church three or four times in our married life. But one night we knew that we had to find some answers or lose our marriage. That night we decided to do something we had never done before. We actually prayed together and asked for help.

"That was just a little step, but it seemed to make a difference. After that, we decided to give church an honest try. So we found one nearby and visited several times. Soon we realized the church was full of people just like us with similar problems, but they had found some real answers. After several weeks, we discovered that the real issue was giving our lives to Christ, not just attending church. I know this may sound overly simple, but it worked.

"For the past five years, this has made a profound difference in our lives. It took a while, but our son Ron finally followed our lead. We have real joy in our home, because we are all headed in the same new direction."

By this time, you have established an openness that will enable you to talk with Jack about how he, too, can give his life to Christ and begin working on his problems.

Sharing Christ Naturally

Someone has said that Jesus' method of witnessing was supernaturally natural. Without a doubt, the major word that should typify our witness is *natural*. Whenever I hear someone beat the drum saying "Witness! Witness!" I become politely annoyed. This is comparable to a man standing by a riverbank shouting, "Flow, river, flow!" You don't need to tell a river to flow, because it does naturally.

Do you and your Timothy like to talk about people you love? You should! That's why I like to tell about Ruth, Heidi, and Heather so much. I love them! A Christian who loves Jesus Christ will find it natural to talk about Him.

If a Christian is not witnessing and sharing his testimony with others, there is something basically wrong, or dammed up, in his Christian life. A spiritually healthy Christian will naturally witness, just as a river will naturally flow.

Scripture in a Testimony

We have dealt with why, when, where, and how. What about Scripture in your testimony? Frequently, ignorance of the verses that explain the plan of salvation or unconfessed sin becomes the dam in a Christian's witnessing experience.

You should have appropriate Scripture verses built into your testimony. Use some selected, well-chosen verses that you have memorized. Teach them to your Timothy. Be sure you have committed them to memory, because you will not always have your Bible with you when you have an opportunity to give a personal testimony.

The Need for Honesty

One of my finest Timothys was a strong, husky young man who is now an evangelist. One day he offered to drive me from Fort Worth to Kerrville, Texas, where I was going to preach. I was physically fatigued at this time, and he was concerned that I might have an auto accident on the way. He also knew this would provide some one-on-one time for study and prayer.

As we were driving along, I asked him to give his testimony. I frequently do this with my Timothys to help them learn to share more effectively.

He said, "Billie, I don't have much of a testimony."

It bothers me to hear any Christian say that. To say you don't have much of a testimony when Jesus Christ saved you from hell and is preparing you for heaven is an unthinking statement. What he meant, of course, was that he'd never been a drug addict, robbed a bank, been immoral, or spent time in jail. I'm glad he didn't have to go through all that to find Christ, but his forgiveness and new life are just as real as the apostle Paul's.

He said, "I was born into a Christian home and became a Christian early in life. Then God led me to a Christian college, where I surrendered for the ministry. There I met a Christian girl, fell in love with her, and married her. Then God led me to seminary, and now I am an evangelist."

In my own gentle way, I looked at him and said, "You liar!"

He was startled. "What? Are you calling me a liar?"

"Why not? You just lied. Don't tell me that phoney story. I want to hear your true testimony." At times, when you are training your Timothy, frankness is the need of the hour.

He looked at me as if shell-shocked. I didn't know what was going to happen next. I said, "Now, go ahead and give me your real testimony."

"It would embarrass me," he replied.

"Now listen. Enough of this sugar-coated stuff. People want to know *why* you became a Christian. So tell them!"

"Well, if you must know, I was a chronic liar from the time I was a little child. My parents couldn't trust me. I couldn't even trust myself. From the time I was a little boy to the time I was converted, I could not tell the truth. I lied all the time."

"Now, I can believe that. That's a story I can handle."

This man had been afraid of being open and honest. The next week he preached in El Paso, Texas, and God led him to give his real testimony. A man in his 40s came up to him at the end of the service and said, "Preacher, is what you just said the truth? About your being a habitual liar?"

He said, "Yes, Sir. I was one, and I couldn't help myself."

The man said, "If God could help you, maybe He could change me as well." And the man was converted that night.

Now, what if my Timothy had gotten up and given his usual bland, incomplete testimony with that poor bleeding man sitting there?

The same need exists in your office, in your home, in your school. People are hurting everywhere, but it doesn't help them to hear about your successes unless they also learn about your failures and how God dealt with them.

Always identify with weaknesses and needs as truthfully as you can, but don't overdo it. If you were immoral, just say that you lived in immorality and avoid the details. You also don't have to pretend to understand a problem if you don't. Don't say, "I was almost a drug addict" when in reality, you were only taking aspirin. Lost people can spot a phoney, and God is never glorified by the sin of exaggeration.

Suggested Assignment

Write out your personal testimony, using the form given at the end of this chapter. Then begin praying for a meaningful opportunity to share with someone this week. Teach your Timothy to do the same, and remember the Lord's promise to give you power to witness through His indwelling Spirit (Acts 1:8). This simple exercise will help you think through your own testimony and prepare you to be used by God.

My Personal Testimony

I. My life before becoming a Christian.

II. How I realized my need for Christ.

III. Why I accepted Christ as my Lord and Savior.

IV. When and how that decision was made.

V. Specific ways Christ has changed my life since I became a Christian.

VI. What the Lord is teaching me now.

5

Sharing God's Plan of Salvation

No human words can adequately describe the price God chose to pay to make forgiveness possible. Spend a moment in meditation, considering the fact that God Himself died to assure our salvation. Ask the Father to let the depth of this amazing truth fill your heart. Ask Him to reemphasize in your mind His eternal Love expressed in His Son. Focus your thoughts on the person of Christ. Notice His radiance, His strength, and His giving yet demanding love. He was like no other man who ever lived, and yet was clearly in every respect fully a man.

To share God's plan of salvation is to share a person—a sinless, victorious, living person. His very name explains His divine mission: ". . . and they shall call His name Immanuel, which translated means, 'God with us'", ". . . for in Him all the fulness of Deity dwells in bodily form . . ." (Matt. 1:23, Col. 2:9 NASB).

He said, "I and the Father are one[1] . . . He who has seen Me, has seen the Father[2] . . . No one has taken [my life] from Me, but I lay it down on My own initiative. I have authority to lay it down, and I have authority to take it up again[3] . . .

[1]John 10:30
[2]John 14:9b
[3]John 10:18

Destroy this temple, and in three days I will raise it up[4] . . .
I am the door; if anyone enters through Me, he shall be saved,
and shall go in and out, and find pasture[5] . . . I am the living
bread that came down out of heaven; if any one eats of this
bread, he shall live forever[6] . . . whoever drinks of the water
that I shall give him shall never thirst; but the water that I
shall give him shall become in him a well of water springing
up to eternal life."[7]

Of Him the Scriptures say: "He is the image of the invisible
God, the first-born of all creation[8] . . . All things came into
being through Him; and apart from Him nothing came into
being[9] . . . both in the heavens and on earth, visible and
invisible, whether thrones or dominions or rulers or authori-
ties—all things have been created through Him and for Him
. . . and in Him all things hold together[10] . . . He was in the
world, and the world was made through Him, but the world
did not know Him.[11] He came to His own, and those who
were His own did not receive Him. But as many as received
Him, to them He gave the right to become children of God,
even to those who believe in His name."[12]

Christ, not religion, not good works, and not world religious
leaders, stands out alone as man's single source of salvation.
Peter explained this to a large crowd after a lame man's ankles
and feet were healed and strengthened in the powerful name
of Jesus Christ. "There is salvation in no one else; for there is
no other name under heaven that has been given among men,

---

[4]John 2:19
[5]John 10:9
[6]John 6:51a
[7]John 4:14
[8]Col. 1:15
[9]John 1:3
[10]Col. 1:16b-17
[11]John 1:10
[12]John 1:11-12

by which we must be saved."[13] Christ was the Father's single and all-sufficient plan for salvation. "For it was the Father's good pleasure for all the fulness to dwell in Him, and through Him to reconcile all things to Himself . . . ."[14]

As you teach your Timothy to share a word of truth and to give his personal testimony, you also need to teach him to present God's plan of salvation in a systematic fashion. Your Timothy must be able to guide a person through the Scriptures so that he can understand *how* to become a Christian.

Faith Produces Boldness

I have always liked the story about the two men in a foxhole. They were totally surrounded by the enemy. John said, "Sam, we're completely surrounded by the enemy; they're everywhere."

Sam replied, "Good! Let's not let a single one of them get away!"

That's the kind of faith and aggressive spirit we need in evangelism. We are surrounded by a sea of need. People everywhere are hungry for Jesus Christ and for salvation, but many of them do not know what label to put on that hunger. They're searching for God, but often they don't even know who or what they are looking for.

Sharing a word of truth gives you and your Timothy an open door to find out a person's level of interest in spiritual things. Your *testimony* reveals the reality of Christ in your own experience. The *plan of salvation* indicates the simple but profound decisions involved in receiving the gift of forgiveness and eternal life.

Philip explained salvation to a complete stranger during the earliest days of the church: "Now an angel of the Lord said to Philip, 'Go south to the road—the desert road—that goes down from Jerusalem to Gaza.' So he started out, and on his way he met an Ethiopian eunuch, an important official in

---

[13] Acts 4:12
[14] Col. 1:19-20a

charge of all the treasury of Candace, queen of the Ethiopians. This man had gone to Jerusalem to worship, and on his way home was sitting in his chariot reading the book of Isaiah the prophet. The Spirit told Philip, 'Go to that chariot and stay near it!'

"Then Philip ran up to the chariot and heard the man reading Isaiah the prophet. 'Do you understand what you are reading?' Philip asked.

" 'How can I,' he said, 'unless someone explains it to me?' So he invited Philip to come up and sit with him" (Acts 8:26-31).

The eunuch did not need a brief general witness about the goodness of God, nor did he need to hear Philip's testimony. What he wanted was a clear understanding of the Christ of Isaiah 53 and the knowledge of how to meet Him as his own Savior. Philip was both available and prepared, and the result was one of the significant conversions of the early church.

Knowing Him Personally

Jesus Christ is not only concerned with getting people interested in Him; He wants them to know Him personally. He wants to redeem them, and He wants them to have a definite conversion experience. This means you have to know how to lead others to an intelligent, forthright decision.

A person doesn't just ooze into Christ. There has to be a moment when he or she says, "Yes, I receive You as my own Lord and Savior."

A person must know that he or she is a Christian and not guess so, hope so, or think so. One of the ways you can help people have this settled assurance is through what has been called the Bridge Illustration. In preparing to present the plan of salvation through the Bridge Illustration, I frequently ask one of these two questions:

(1) Do you think about spiritual things often?

(2) Through the years have you come to know Christ personally, or are you still on the way?

This approach gently opens the door for explaining the Bridge Illustration.

The Bridge Illustration

Let's assume you are talking with someone who is interested and eager to listen. Get a sheet of paper (even a napkin will do) and write on it: "MAN" and "GOD" (Fig. 1). Explain that "Man has always wanted to know God and in a variety of ways has sought to worship Him."

Share the fact that there is a serious problem that keeps us from having the quality relationship with God that we really need and that He wants us to have. The Bible tells us about that problem in Romans 3:23—"For all have sinned and fall short of the glory of God."

Hand the person a Bible, point to that verse, and ask him to read it aloud to you. People do not want to hear your opinion about Jesus Christ. They want to see what the Bible says. The average person has a profound respect for the Bible, even though he may never have read it. Let the Scripture speak for itself.

After he has read the verse, carry on a conversation something like this: "Now, William, that verse you have just read says all have sinned. What does it say about you? Are you part of that *all*?"

MAN   GOD

Fig. 1

"Yeah, I'm part of that *all*."

"Well, what does it say about you?"

"It says that I've sinned."

If he inquires about the rest of the verse, say, "William, 'Fallen short of the glory of God' means living a life that is imperfect. All of us have lived lives that are sinful and unlike that of Jesus Christ. His life was sinless and perfect, and all the world has fallen short of that standard."

It has been the author's experience that no one seems to feel his life measures up to that of Jesus. Therefore, they understand the concept of sin once this comparison has been made.

Write the reference "Rom. 3:23" under "MAN," and write "*All* Have Sinned" next to it. Then draw in the chasm between "MAN" and "GOD" and write "SIN" in that space. (Fig. 2).

Now turn to Romans 6:23 and have him read the verse aloud. "For the wages of sin is death; but the gift of God is eternal life in Christ Jesus our Lord." The word "wages" needs some explanation. I usually say something like this, "William, have you ever worked for wages?"

He replies, "Yes, I have a job."

"All right, what is a wage?"

"It's the salary you earn. It's what you get on payday."

"The Bible says that sin earns death. When payday comes,

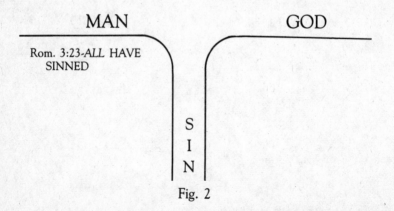

Fig. 2

death is what you will have earned. When a man sins and is separated from God, he is dead toward God and has no relationship with his Creator. So all have sinned, and because of your sin, you have earned spiritual death."

"William, two kinds of death are explained in the Bible. One is physical, which we're going to look at in a moment, and the other is spiritual, which the Bible is talking about here."

At this point pause to write down "Rom. 6:23" in your illustration and the words, "Sin *Earns* Death" next to it (Fig. 3).

Next, turn to Hebrews 9:27 and let him read aloud—"Man is destined to die once, and after that to face judgment."

Say, "This verse speaks of physical death. God has appointed a time when every man, woman, boy and girl will die physically. Our brief time here on earth is to prepare for that all-important day. Only God knows when it will come.

"William, some day you're going to die, and so will I. After that we will face God's judgment. When we look at the facts, mankind has a real problem that adds up to eternal death."

Now write "Heb. 9:27" under the other verses with the notation "All die *physically*" by it. Then summarize the results of these three verses in the words "eternal death" (Fig 4). At this point you have clearly demonstrated William's condition.

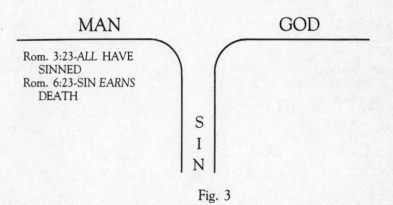

MAN   GOD

Rom. 3:23-*ALL* HAVE
   SINNED
Rom. 6:23-SIN *EARNS*
   DEATH

S
I
N

Fig. 3

Now you will be able to help him see the wonderful plan made possible by Christ's love. Begin with Romans 5:8—"But God demonstrates his own love for us in this: While we were still sinners, Christ died for us." Emphasize the fact that God took the initiative while we were still guilty of our sin.

"William, you are in the midst of your sin, but God loves you just as you are."

On the right side of your illustration under "GOD" write "Rom. 5:8" and by it the words "Christ died for us while we were still sinners." Then draw a cross, bridging the gap between "GOD" and "MAN" (Fig. 5). This is why Jesus went to the cross: to pay the penalty of our sin, so mark through the word, "sin."

Then turn to Ephesians 2:8, 9—"For it is by grace you have been saved, through faith—and this is not from yourselves, it is the gift of God—not by works, so that no one can boast."

"William, it is by God's grace and love that we are able to become Christians. It is a love you don't deserve and a love you can never earn. If a gift is offered that must then be earned, it isn't a gift. And salvation is something God gives us because He loves us. It is strictly a gift."

I once tested this with my secretary. I called her into my

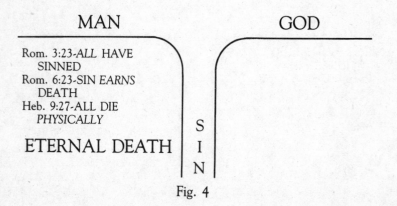

Fig. 4

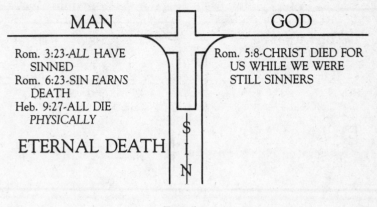

Fig. 5

office and said, "If I were to give you your paycheck in a gift-wrapped box, what would be your immediate response?"

She answered, "Real disappointment. I would open the gift thinking it was a bonus—something extra special. Then I would discover it was only my paycheck. I would think, *Are you hinting that I haven't been earning my wages? Why would you consider my paycheck a gift?*"

Explain to your inquirer that salvation is a gift from God, which cannot be received on the basis of merit.

Write "Eph. 2:8-9" on the right side and by it the words "By God's love we are saved through faith" (Fig. 6).

Next turn to John 1:12 and ask your friend to read this verse to you—"Yet to all who received him, to those who believed in his name, he gave the right to become children of God." Pay close attention to the two key words—*believe* and *receive*.

Now say, "William, there are two steps in this verse that explain how to become a child of God. The first is to believe in Jesus Christ. You must honestly accept that He is who He claimed to be. Do you believe that He was born of a virgin, that He lived a sinless life, that He died for your sins, and that

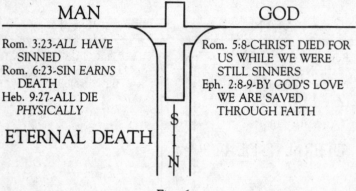

Fig. 6

He rose from the grave in victory? If you do, you will be eager to take the second step, which is to receive Him as your own Savior and Lord."

(In the final analysis, you are leading William to see that Jesus is God and that his decision about Jesus means accepting or rejecting God. Intellectual acceptance is not enough. The act of faith must occur for the rebirth to be experienced. William must exercise his will to receive Christ into his life.)

At this point, draw a bridge across the top of the cross on your diagram, and write "Believe and Receive" and "John 1:12" over the top of the bridge; also write "Eternal Life" on the right side (Fig. 7).

To illustrate the difference between believing and receiving, take a pen or pencil and ask, "William, do you believe that I have a pen in my hand?"

"Yes, I do."

"Well, do you believe it enough that if I offer it to you, you will take it?" You offer it, and he takes it.

Now ask, "William, what did you just do?"

"I took it."

"Why did you take it?"

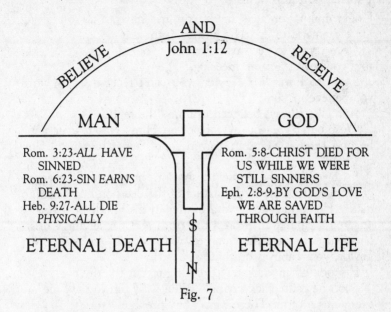

Fig. 7

"Because you offered it to me."

"In other words, you believed me when I said I would give it to you, so you were willing to reach out to receive it."

He responds, "That's right."

"William, the pen was yours potentially the moment I decided to offer it, but it wasn't yours *experientially* until you acted in faith and received it.

"What Christ did on the cross was potentially for everyone in the world. The gift has already been paid for, and the loving hand of God is now extended. He is simply waiting for you and every other person to believe in Him enough to receive His gift that He offered in the Person of Christ."

(Because I am typically drawing the Bridge Illustration on a piece of paper with a pen or pencil, this is my favorite way to explain John 1:12. Others have used a stick in the sand or their finger in the dust to get the same truth across.)

Unusual Circumstances

Under unusual circumstances, you may have to do something more dramatic to drive home the truth.

I was trying to get this point across one day in West Texas to a cowboy at a camp meeting.

I said to him, "Mr. Taylor, you can't receive Christ until you believe in Him."

"Oh, I've always believed in Him," he replied.

"Yes, but have you ever received Him? Has it ever gone beyond 'there is a God in heaven,' and, 'Yes, Christ is the Son of God'?"

I showed him the Bridge Illustration, but I couldn't seem to get him to understand the nature of the decision he needed to make. He seemed to have a barrier in his mind. So I finally enacted a parable to express the truth about receiving Christ. I looked out across the camp toward his cabin and said, "Mr. Taylor, your cabin is on fire."

He took off immediately, running to put the fire out.

Soon he came back saying, "Billie, why did you tell me my cabin was on fire? There wasn't any fire."

I said, "I just wanted to illustrate the verse we were talking about—the one about believing and receiving."

"What do you mean?"

"Did you believe what I said about the fire?"

"Sure I believed you! I went to put the fire out."

"All right, Mr. Taylor, let me show you something. A few minutes ago you said you believed in the Lord Jesus Christ, yet you have refused to pray and receive Him as your Lord. True belief requires action. Mr. Taylor, the day you truly believe in Jesus Christ, you will have no option but to pray and receive Him as your Lord and your God. Until that time, you may admire Him, respect Him, and even fear Him, but according to the Bible you do not really believe in Him until you receive Him."

Dealing With Self-Worth

In sharing the plan of salvation, you will discover that most people fall into one of two categories. One doesn't believe God is *adequate* to save them. The other doesn't believe they are *worth* saving. Many times it is helpful for them to see this difference themselves.

I first learned the importance of this fact while talking to a lost geologist who truly wanted to be saved. After we talked for some time, I finally said, "Let's assume I am with Exxon, and I have come to offer you a million-dollar retainer, because we feel you are such a brilliant geologist. I want you to be available to our geological staff. We don't want you to do any specific work, we just want you to be available for future consultation. On that basis, would you take the check?"

"You bet, I'd take it!"

"Do you think the check would bounce?"

"Of course not. That's why I would take it."

He believed in the financial strength of Exxon; therefore, he would gladly take the check.

I said, "Mr. Wright, do you believe that God is strong enough to forgive your sins?"

"I never thought about it like that," he replied. "I do believe that He's that powerful."

"All right, then, what you are saying is that you already have faith in Exxon and you want to have faith in God. Mr. Wright, there are only two reasons why an honest man would not take the Exxon retainer. The first would be that he didn't believe that Exxon was worth the money, and you have negated that. The second would be that you don't believe you are worth the amount of the retainer. Is that why you haven't received Jesus Christ?"

His look of surprise was followed by the dawn of understanding. It was deeply fulfilling to observe the change in his countenance as he realized that his feelings of low self-worth had been the elusive barrier that had hindered him in his desire to know God. After discussing Romans 5:8 again, warm tears were followed by an earnest decision to receive Christ.

Countless millions of people are just outside the kingdom waiting to be assured that in God's eyes they are *worth* saving.

Now return to your completed diagram (Fig. 7) and ask the person to whom you are witnessing, "William, where are you on this diagram? Are you on the left side (MAN) or are you on the right (GOD)? Or somewhere in between?"

When that question is asked, the average person will put his finger in the middle, on the "AND" between "BELIEVE" and "RECEIVE." He has not understood how to commit himself. He will often say, "Yes, I believe in Christ, but no, I've never personally received Him as my Savior."

Many good, moral people have an intellectual belief in Christ but have never committed themselves to receiving Him. Actually, when they put their finger on the "AND" in the middle, they have helped you recognize exactly where they are.

You can now say to the person, "Wonderful! William, you've taken the first step; you already believe in Christ. Now wouldn't you like to finish it? Wouldn't you like to take the next step and actually receive Him into your life?"

The usual answer is, "Yes, I would. No one's ever explained how before."

The next step is a prayer, which I call the Sinner's Prayer.

The Sinner's Prayer

After a person has seen his need of conversion, it is a dangerous thing to leave him without help in the area of prayer. Over the years, I have learned there is much value in memorizing the seven basic elements to a sinner's prayer. Learn these, so that when God gives you someone who is ready to receive Him, you will be prepared.

The seven ingredients are confession, contrition, repentance, invitation, consecration, dependence, and thanksgiving. (You will find the first five of these elements in the Parable of the Prodigal Son—Luke 15:11-32, particularly verses 17-21.) The words for each section are:

1. Confession—"Lord Jesus, I am a sinner."
2. Contrition—"But I am sorry for my sins."
3. Repentance—"I want to turn from my sins; I am willing to begin a new life with Your help."
4. Invitation—"Lord Jesus, please come into my heart and life right now."

5. Consecration—"From this moment forward, my life belongs to You and You alone."

6. Dependence—"I will love You, serve You, and tell others about You, and trust You to live Your life through me."

7. Thanksgiving—"Thank You, Lord, for coming into my life and for forgiving my sins today."

After you pray a prayer like that with a person, the next thing you should do is show him 1 John 5:11-13—"And this is the testimony: God has given us eternal life, and this life is in his Son. He who has the Son has life; he who does not have the Son of God does not have life. I write these things to you who believe in the name of the Son of God so that you may *know* that you have eternal life."

This lets the inquirer know what the Bible says about the assurance he can have regarding his decision and prayer to receive Christ.

For some who are reading this book, this might be the most important section as you consider your own life. Come to a deep assurance concerning the promise of these verses. I have never met a powerful witness who did not have an equally solid conviction concerning the assurance of his salvation in Christ.

Assurance is more than a feeling. It is an unshakable, eternal promise. "He who has the Son has life." If you do not have this assurance, read the sinner's prayer, slowly and thoughtfully. If you have never been sure in the past, let today seal this matter for eternity. Ask Christ into your heart, and begin to thank Him that from this moment forward you can know beyond question that you have eternal life.

Salvation Understood

On the joyous occasion when a child is born physically into the world, it knows nothing about genes or its own formation. Yet it experiences the full blessing of life.

In a similar way, when an individual experiences rebirth and becomes part of the spiritual family of God, there is much he or she does not understand about salvation. This is one of the reasons why followup and nurture are so important.

One night after a crusade service, I joined two friends for dinner at a small cafe. During our meal, the Lord brought a couple to my attention. They were sitting at a booth only three tables away. When I finished eating, I went to their table and introduced myself. We talked about the direction of their lives and their need for a personal relationship with God. About two hours later, they reverently bowed their heads and each prayed to receive Christ.

It was only after our prayer that John told me he was the lead guitarist at Houston's foremost nightclub. He and Kathy had been dating for some time and their lives had revolved around the nightclub circuit. Almost immediately, the question was raised concerning how God would view John's future employment at the club.

The next evening, he and Kathy were our special guests at the crusade, where he played the guitar. We also had the 150-voice youth choir of the First Baptist Church of Dallas. It was an unforgettable evening, but there were still many questions in John and Kathy's minds. Knowing that I would have to leave the city within a day or two, I contacted a pastor who was a good friend and asked him to follow them up personally to ensure their spiritual well-being and growth. He faithfully followed through and provided individual help for both of them, as well as giving them a great deal of pastoral guidance. After two years of instruction, the Lord led John and Kathy to surrender their lives for vocational Christian service.

The most difficult hurdle they faced during their early Christian pilgrimage had to do with the proper understanding of salvation. Several of their relatives belonged to a group that teaches that an individual must be baptized by immersion in order to receive salvation.

These sincere but confused relatives continued to cast doubt on the conversion experience of John and Kathy and their subsequent baptism. They insisted that salvation did not occur unless they were baptized in their particular group and for the specific purpose of salvation, rather than because of salvation. After many discussions with their pastor, John and Kathy not only came to a firm assurance of their relationship with God through the grace and love of Jesus Christ, but were also able to help others.

Facets of Salvation

If I had been available to John and Kathy during their early Christian growth, and if I had known what I do today, I would have shared several things with them from the Scriptures. To begin with, I would have led them to understand that conversion is like a beautiful diamond that possesses numerous facets:

From *God the Father's* perspective, at the moment of salvation you become His child. "But as many as received Him, to them He gave the right to become children of God, even to those who believe in His name" (John 1:12 NASB).

From the perspective of *God the Son,* He becomes your Lord. "That if you confess with your mouth Jesus as Lord, and believe in your heart that God raised Him from the dead, you shall be saved; for with the heart man believes, resulting in righteousness, and with the mouth he confesses, resulting in salvation" (Rom. 10:9, 10 NASB).

From the perspective of *God the Spirit,* salvation means that He has baptized you into the Body of Christ, which is His Church. "For by one Spirit we were all baptized into one body, whether Jews or Greeks, whether slaves or free, and we were all made to drink of one Spirit" (1 Cor. 12:13 NASB).

From the perspective of the *sinner,* salvation means the assurance that your sins have been forgiven. "Of Him all the prophets bear witness that through His name everyone who believes in Him receives forgiveness of sin" (Acts 10:43 NASB).

To *the witness* who has shared Christ, salvation means converting a sinner from the error of his ways. "Let him know that he who turns a sinner from the error of his way will save his soul from death, and will cover a multitude of sins" (James 5:20 NASB).

The single act of receiving Christ is referred to in the Scriptures as being born again spiritually, being justified, reconciled, redeemed, adopted by God, and many other descriptive terms that stand for the same experience.

I would then have shown John and Kathy Ephesians 1:13, which says, ". . . after listening to the message of truth, the gospel of your salvation—having also believed, you were sealed in Him with the Holy Spirit of promise," emphasizing the fact that when the Holy Spirit came into their hearts, His presence was a pledge that they would have a place in heaven.

Saving Faith

After this general explanation, I would help them understand the *sequence of events* as seen in the Scriptures when the first group of Gentiles found Christ. We would read chapter 10 of the Book of Acts together, making note of the careful leadership of the Spirit of God in bringing Cornelius to the place where he was willing to send for the Apostle Peter. I would also emphasize that God the Holy Spirit had to deal with Peter so he would understand that God is not one to show partiality (10:43).

Referring back to 1 Corinthians 12:13, we would discuss the fact that God was teaching the early church that both Jews and Gentiles, whether slaves or free, all became Christians in exactly the same manner. They were baptized by the Holy Spirit into one unified Body at the moment of conversion.

Looking at Romans 8:9-11, I would show that the Spirit of God lives in the believer and that a Christian belongs to Jesus Christ by virtue of that fact. "You are not in the flesh but in the Spirit, if indeed the Spirit of God dwells in you. But if anyone does not have the Spirit of Christ, he does not belong to Him. . . . But if the Spirit of Him who raised Jesus from the dead dwells in you, He who raised Christ Jesus from the dead will also give life to your mortal bodies through His Spirit who indwells you" (NASB).

Turning back to the narrative of Cornelius' house in Acts 10, we would study verse 43. For it was while Peter was saying these words, "Everyone who believes in him receives forgiveness of sins," that the Holy Spirit fell on the Gentiles who were listening to the sermon. The moment their faith was turned toward Christ, the Holy Spirit fell on them, baptizing them into the Body of Christ.

The immediate response of Peter and the six Jewish men who accompanied him was one of amazement. Peter immediately said, "Can anyone keep these people from being baptized with water? They have received the Holy Spirit just as we have. So he ordered that they be baptized in the name of Jesus Christ" (10:47-48).

In summary, I would point out that forgiveness of sins, which means salvation, was conditioned on their belief in Jesus Christ. Simultaneously with their initial belief, they received God's regenerating Holy Spirit. It was on the basis of their salvation and the obvious fact that God was no respecter of persons that Peter ordered them to be baptized with water in the name of the Lord Jesus Christ.

Clearly, when these first Gentiles were baptized with water, it was not so that they would be saved, but because they had already experienced salvation as the result of their response to the witness of Peter and their faith in the person of Jesus Christ.

To ensure beyond question their understanding of this important teaching of the Scriptures, I would take John and Kathy to Acts 15, to an event that occurred several years later in the Council in Jerusalem. Beginning in verse 7 and reading through verse 11, I would allow them to listen to the apostle Peter recount the story of the conversion of the early Gentiles at Cornelius' house. In verse 11 they would learn that we are saved in the same way as those early Gentiles. And how does that salvation come? Not by water baptism, but by the Holy Spirit cleansing our hearts *by faith.* Peter clearly states, "We believe that we are saved through the grace of the Lord Jesus, in the same way as they also are" (15:11 NASB).

Scriptural Obedience

Before closing our session together, I would do two more things. First, I would emphasize the importance of water baptism as a joyful act of obedience in identification with Jesus Christ. Then I would point out the individual verses like:

"And Peter said to them, 'Repent, and let each of you be baptized in the name of Jesus Christ for the forgiveness of your sins; and you shall receive the gift of the Holy Spirit' " (Acts 2:38 NASB).

"He saved us, not on the basis of deeds which we have done in righteousness, but according to His mercy, by the washing of regeneration and renewing by the Holy Spirit" (Titus 3:5 NASB).

"And corresponding to that, baptism now saves you—not the removal of dirt from the flesh, but an appeal to God for a good conscience—through the resurrection of Jesus Christ" (1 Peter 3:21).

These verses need to be understood in the light of those studied in Acts 10 and their summary in Acts 11:14-18, where once again it is the Holy Spirit's baptism that marked their conversion, rather than baptism with water.

In John and Kathy's case, Acts 2:38 was the primary verse that was being emphasized by their relatives in isolation from other passages on the subject of salvation. With regard to that question, it is important to note that the only place in the New Testament where the question, "What must I do to be saved?" (Acts 16:30) is asked, Paul and Silas both replied, "Believe in the Lord Jesus, and you will be saved" (16:31). So specifically inspired was this answer that they both prophesied that the family of the jailer would also believe on Christ and be saved.

As Paul and Silas explained the Word of the Lord to this gentile family, that prophecy was fulfilled. The jailer's family believed and the condition for salvation was met, just as it was for the family of Cornelius.

Notice, however, that in both instances, these gentile families were immediately willing and eager to be baptized. In neither of these early gentile conversions is there any suggestion that water baptism is a condition for salvation.

Judaism to Completed Judaism

In Acts 2:37-38 the Jewish audience listening to Peter cried out a much broader question than this Philippian jailer. They did not ask, "What must we do to be saved?" but rather, "What shall we do?" (2:37)

Peter responded with an equally broad answer that must be understood in the light of the rest of the Book of Acts. He forcefully called those who had crucified Christ to *repent* of all their sin. Luke says that *devout* men from many nations were in the crowd (Acts 2:5 NASB). In an Old Testament sense, these individuals were *already saved* through their personal faith in Jehovah and His covenant with Abraham—that the Messiah would come.[15] Their question makes it obvious that they already believed what Peter was saying. Now, they wanted to know what to do.

It must be remembered that nearly two months had passed since the Lord's crucifixion, and some of those present had only recently arrived in the city to celebrate the Jewish Feast of Pentecost. They had not heard Jesus preach, seen Him heal, or rejected Him.

Peter's anointed message came to them as new information. Three thousand present readily accepted Peter's words. They did this out of a sense of deep conviction that the Jewish religious structure and community at large had rejected their Messiah.

Based upon their faith, Peter instructed each Jew to demonstrate the sincerity of his repentance in the manner that had been common to both John the Baptist and the disciples of Jesus—water baptism. Throughout all the Gospels, Jesus had emphasized repentance, not water baptism, as the prerequisite for forgiveness. Now Peter did the same. The promise of the Father, which is the gift of the Holy Spirit, was never related to water baptism.

---

[15]See fuller explanation in Appendix 3.

The emphasis of the New Testament is summarized by the apostle Paul in his famous words in the epistle to the Romans: "[This] is the word of faith which we are preaching, that if you confess with your mouth Jesus as Lord, and believe in your heart that God raised Him from the dead, you shall be saved; for with the heart man believes, resulting in righteousness, and with the mouth he confesses, resulting in salvation. For the Scripture says, 'Whoever believes in Him will not be disappointed.' For there is no distinction between Jew and Greek; for the same Lord is Lord of all, abounding in riches for all who call upon Him" (Rom. 10:8b-12 NASB).

In the final analysis, I want John and Kathy to understand that God looks on the sincerity of the heart and that "whoever will call upon the name of the Lord will be saved."

6

Principles From Witness Encounters

We have the opportunity to introduce people to God, but we do not have the power to regenerate or to convert them. That is the sacred work of the Holy Spirit. Conversion is the prerogative of God. But He has committed the ministry of reconciliation or evangelism to us. "All this is from God, who reconciled us to himself through Christ and gave us the ministry of reconciliation: that God was reconciling the world to himself in Christ, not counting men's sins against them. And he has committed to us the message of reconciliation" (2 Cor. 5:18-19).

Since evangelism is bringing people to the place where they know and love God in Jesus Christ, every witness must realize that the one with whom he shares has the capacity to say yes or no to this divine relationship. We must teach our Timothys to learn from each witnessing experience, just as a fisherman becomes proficient at his skill by years of diligent effort and experience. In all our witnessing, we should constantly ask ourselves these questions: What should I have learned? What did I do right? What did I do wrong? How can I allow God to use me more effectively? As you evaluate your witnessing encounters, principles will emerge that will become lifelong companions during your personal ministry. In this chapter we will look at some witness encounters and draw some principles from them.

Leslie

The young woman seated at my right at a wedding rehearsal dinner in Phoenix, Arizona, was a UCLA dental hygiene student. About halfway through the meal, she quietly whispered to me, "You know, there's something very peculiar about the people at this table."

I looked around and saw that except for this young woman, all the people at our table were good friends of mine. I knew all of them well. I couldn't help but wonder what would be so peculiar about my friends. So I stopped eating and thought, "What would they have in common that would seem strange to her?" Then it dawned on me that everyone at the table was a dedicated follower of Jesus Christ. I knew nothing about her faith.

Following my hunch, I said to her, "I believe I know what is so peculiar about everyone at this table, but it's a secret."

Having said this, I began to eat again. She leaned over and said to me urgently, "I've got to know. What makes these people so different?"

I replied, "Well, I can tell you, but I can only do it in private, whenever we have the time to talk."

"All right. I want to know."

At the end of the meal she was right there, tugging at my coat sleeve, saying, "Don't forget you promised to tell me the secret."

So we went out to the front porch of the Ramada Inn where we could talk quietly. I explained, "The thing that is so peculiar about the people at our table is that without exception, Jesus Christ lives inside their bodies."

She exclaimed, "Who lives in their bodies?"

I replied, "Jesus Christ. That is why they are so different from other people."

She said, "Well, I just never heard of such a thing."

"Leslie, we are part of a group that's pretty well known all over the world. We are called Christians. We are disciples of Jesus Christ and have invited Him to live in our bodies."

She looked at me with great amazement and said, "I'm a Methodist. Does that count?"

I replied, "It might. Then again it might not. Many people who go to church are searching but are not yet really Christians. The Bible says that if you do not have the Spirit of Christ, then you do not belong to Him (Rom. 8:9). So to become a Christian and belong to Him, you must invite Him to come live in you. Though He wants to do this, He cannot and will not enter your life until you honestly repent of your sins.

She looked at me with a great deal of pride. A little bit of anger flashed across her face as she said, "Never once have I committed a sin. I don't have to worry about that."

"How old are you?" I asked.

"I'm nineteen."

"Do you mean to tell me that you've never done anything wrong in all your nineteen years?"

"Never! Furthermore, you seem like a nice person, and I seriously doubt that you're a sinner either."

"Leslie," I said, "speak for yourself. I know my heart, and I know that I have done and thought many things that have grieved God. Sometimes I have to deal with sin daily, sometimes hourly."

She looked totally shocked.

I continued, "Leslie, if you will get on your knees with me right now and tell God that you've never committed a sin, never done anything wrong, nothing selfish or impure—if He will believe you and accept your prayer, then I will certainly believe it, too."

With a look of egotism, she said, "Me? Get on my knees?"

I replied, "Leslie, are you unwilling to get on your knees in front of Almighty God?"

She walked off the porch, turned to me and asked, "Is pride a sin?"

I said, "It'll do."

She fell on her knees on the grass, disregarding her beautiful pastel dress, and began to pray. "O God, forgive me. I am Your creation, yet I was too proud and arrogant to get on my knees before You. Please forgive me for the sin of pride that has kept Jesus Christ out of my life. Lord, please come into me right now and let me be one of these 'peculiar' people."

She received Christ and His forgiveness on that lawn and was wonderfully converted! She witnessed to one of her relatives that night, and with the help of a mutual Christian friend, she developed into an extremely effective, witnessing Christian.

When her life ended unexpectedly only two years later, she left behind a radiant Christian testimony that positively affected the lives of scores of people.

Insights gained:

—it was contact with *winsome Christians* that made her want to know what made these people so different. She detected in them the character, the aroma, of Christ

—their *transparent happiness* was obvious, and yet she could not understand why

—she had to *realize her need* before she could receive help

—when she did decide to become a Christian, she *knew why,* and she immediately *wanted to share* her good news with others

—the privilege of *apprenticeship* under a more experienced Christian provided her with the stability and fellowship that she needed to become an effective spiritual witness.

Principles to note:

1) In sharing Christ, whet the appetite of a person so he or she will *want* to hear your testimony. In this instance, I used secretiveness for that purpose.

2) Find a *specific sin* and deal with it. In Leslie's case, her real problem was pride.

Thor

I was flying from Australia to New Zealand, seated next to a young man who had shown some interest in Christ when we talked a short while at the airport. We had decided to sit together on the plane.

He was with a group of surfers—the top twenty of the world—who were traveling together while making a movie about international surfboarding.

As we were talking, the supervisor of the group, a man named Thor, noticed that we were having a serious conversation. He was an atheist, as I discovered later. He came over to our seats and said abruptly, "Sir, this young man is on my surfboarding team and under my authority, and I want him to go and sit in my seat."

I thought this somewhat odd until Thor sat down in the vacated seat and said, "I don't believe in the Bible. I don't believe in sin, and I don't want to hear your testimony."

I just opened my Bible to John 3:16, laid it in his lap, pointed to the verse, and said, "Is this what you don't believe?"

He silently read the verse, "For God so loved the world that He gave his one and only Son, that whoever believes in him shall not perish but have eternal life," and said, "That's the very verse I don't like."

"What is it you don't like about this verse?"

"I don't like your interpretation of it."

In a polite tone of voice, I replied, "But I haven't interpreted it yet!"

He began to laugh when he realized that I hadn't said a word. So I said, "Thor, you don't have to be afraid of me. I am just like all other Christians. I've come to personally know Christ and He has brought real joy into my life."

As we began talking, I said, "Thor, everyone has a god. What do you worship?"

"My god is my surfboard," he replied.

"What happens when your surfboard gets broken on the rocks?"

"I just go out and buy another one. I live for surfing. That's all that really matters to me."

I've discovered that when you are talking to an atheist like Thor, you need to ask questions tactfully that are related to his family or personal life. That's where you'll be able to discover some tender areas where help is needed.

When I brought the subject around to his family, Thor informed me that he was divorced and miserable. Tears formed in his eyes. God confronted him, and he was under conviction. The issue was quite simple: "You've failed in your marriage, and your surfboard couldn't help you."

Thor didn't pray to receive Christ, but I didn't necessarily expect him to do so that quickly. I had the joy of knowing, however, that I had been faithful and that God was dealing with him. It was obvious he was beginning to realize his spiritual need.

Over the years I have prayed for Thor on many occasions and trust that in this world or the next I will have the privilege of meeting him again. It has been my consistent prayer that I will meet a brother in Christ on that occasion.

Principles to note:

1) The principle we see in this encounter is that whenever someone says he *does not believe in the Bible,* you should ask specifically which verses he rejects. Use your Bible and discuss those verses together. As you read, the Holy Spirit will be faithful to convict him of sin, just as Jesus promised.

2) When possible, move beyond his intellectual questions to his *personal need.*

Abdul

In Calcutta, India, where I was mildly sick to my stomach, I ordered a very bland chicken dinner (definitely no curry!). Somewhere between the kitchen and my hotel room, someone stole the chicken. All I received was a beautiful silver plate with potatoes and tomatoes on it.

I called the kitchen and said, "My chicken is missing! I have the potatoes and tomatoes, but no chicken."

They apologized profusely and promised to send me another.

The waiter knocked loudly. As I opened the door, he thrust forth his right hand and took mine and shook it vigorously. He almost shouted, "Hello. I'm Abdul, a *Muslim!*"

In spite of how sick I felt, I mustered all my strength and firmly gripped his hand, forcefully replying, "I'm Hanks, a Christian!"

Fortunately, he didn't drop the chicken.

There we were, two fanatics, staring at each other eye to eye. After I asked him to come in, he placed the chicken on the table. My Bible was lying open on the bed.

He asked, "Is that your Holy Book?"

"Yes, it is," I replied.

"May I see it?"

"Please do," and I turned to the Gospel of John, chapter 3.

Reading aloud about Jesus and Nicodemus, he stopped after verse 3: "Unless a man is born again, he cannot see the kingdom of God."

He asked, "What does it mean to be born again?"

Three hours later, Abdul gave his life to Jesus Christ.

Between his original question and the time he received Christ, I carefully explained the plan of salvation, emphasizing that Jesus is the only way to God.

As an illustration of the adequacy of Christ, I asked him to climb up on my back. Then I said, "Look down and imagine that there is a dark chasm, and you have not found the way to cross it. Pretend that I am Jesus and that I am the only One who can carry you safely to God. Jesus said, 'I am the Way, the Truth, and the Life, and no one comes to the Father but by me.' Abdul, you must trust in Him alone to deliver you from the consequences of sin and carry you safely into the presence of the Father."

God made this so vivid, Abdul was almost frightened as I stepped out on an imaginary tightrope to carry him across the chasm.

"This is what you've got to do," I explained. "In order to be saved from the judgment of sin, you've got to get on Jesus' back!"

He said, "I think there is something like this in the Koran."

"I don't know if this example is in the Koran," I replied, "but Jesus Christ is the only One who can get you across that chasm that separates man and God. Muhammad can't do it, and he never said he could. He never claimed divinity or said that he had the power to forgive sin. But Jesus said He could. Trust in Jesus and let Him carry you across to forgiveness of sin and eternal life."

After we had discussed his remaining questions about the Trinity and salvation through faith, we prayed earnestly together. A radiance came over his countenance, and he said, "This is the greatest thing that has ever happened to me. This is what I've been looking for all my life. I've got to go and tell my friends."

You can imagine my surprise when he said, "I'm a member of the Communist Party, and we have a meeting tonight. They will be so surprised when I tell them what has happened to me!"

Before he left my room, we had decided where he would worship the following Sunday morning.

Principles to note:

1) Abdul's conversion is a good example of the importance of bringing a lost individual into direct contact with the Word of God. When possible, always allow the inquirer to hold the Bible and *read it for himself.*

2) Remember that Jesus *illustrated the truth* of the gospel through the use of parables. When applicable, do not hesitate to paint a picture physically or verbally to get your point across.

3) After a decision is made and the inquirer comes to assurance of salvation, help him or her make specific plans to *follow through* with church membership and Christian fellowship.

Two Hitchhikers

At one point in my life, God was putting me through the school of usability. I had asked Him to use me in evangelism, but I soon learned that could occur only on His terms. "For it is God who works in you to will and to act according to his good purpose" (Phil. 2:13). His terms include His way, His timing, and His wording.

While driving to my apartment in Waco, Texas, one Saturday night, I passed a couple walking down the opposite side of the highway, hitchhiking.

The Lord spoke to my heart, "Billie, pick them up. I want to use you."

"I must be talking to myself," I thought. "Surely this couldn't be God speaking to me. First, I don't pick up hitchhikers; second, it's nighttime; third, it's a couple; fourth, they are going in the opposite direction." There were four logical reasons for me not to pick them up.

So I prayed about it, and said, "Lord, if this is really You, I am willing to go back. I do want to be used, but please make it unmistakably clear."

"Go back," came the still, small voice in my heart.

Whenever you are praying, "Lord, do You really want me to witness to that person?" stop and say, "God, if it's really You, impress it on me so *hard* that I can't miss it. If it's not You, then take the impression away altogether."

Satan is an accuser and will try to make you feel guilty for not having witnessed, but God is willing and completely able to reveal His specific will to you in answer to your request for a strong impression.

I drove on, but God impressed it on me so hard that I turned around, went back, and picked them up. Sticking their heads in the window, they asked, "Where are you going?"

"Anywhere you are," I replied.

My answer scared them, so they asked me to explain.

I said. "It'll be hard for you to understand. I was going in the opposite direction but felt impressed that I should pick you up." Obviously, this started the conversation in the right direction.

They were going to a house in another part of the city, so I was able to spend about thirty minutes with them. By the time we'd pulled up in their driveway, both had prayed to receive Christ.

Principles to note:

1) When you are seeking to be fully involved in a life of

obedience, you can be assured that *adventure* will accompany your desire.

2) You must remember God is *sovereign* and that you cannot always predict what He is going to do. When God does something spontaneous in your life, do not necessarily expect Him to repeat it. He will not normally have you do the same things in the same way each time you witness.

Teenage Gang

One evening as I prepared to preach, God was again putting me through the school of obedience.

I felt a strong impression to walk down the street next to my apartment. I knew the Lord was aware of my fear of dogs, but the Holy Spirit's tugging persisted. He definitely wanted something done down that dark street.

Leaving the apartment, I walked down the center stripe on the road. The dogs were barking in the yards on both sides. Some ran out, as if they were going to attack me. A friend had shown me a technique to make dogs think you had a stick in your hand when you didn't, so I went through all the gymnastics of trying to make the dogs think I had a stick. I made it for one full block, dodging dogs all the way, and not a one of them bit me. I felt like Daniel in a dog's den!

At the end of the block there was a junior high school, with a baseball diamond. I began to walk the bases preaching out loud, rehearsing my sermon for the next day. This went on for about thirty minutes.

Suddenly, by the school, I noticed five very small lights.

I thought, "That's an odd thing. It must be a reflection or something." Then I thought, "Perhaps someone is robbing the school. No, that isn't likely."

So I kept on walking and preaching. Then the small lights became brighter and moved closer. After a while, it became clear to me that there were five figures behind those lights and that the lights were cigarettes.

A voice came out of the darkness and said, "Man, don't you know it isn't safe to be out here alone at night?"

Instantly, the Lord gave me assurance and the words to say. With great authority, I replied, "I AM NOT ALONE!"

The five teenage gang members got in a semicircle around me and one of them said, "Who's with you?"

"The Lord is with me!"

"*Who?*"

"The Lord is with me!"

As soon as I said that, I sat down and looked up. "Don't you have any manners at all? Be seated!"

The boys were so shocked, they didn't know what to do. Quietly they sat in a circle. One said, "Man, are you crazy or something?"

"No, I'm not crazy. I'm the pastor of the First Baptist Church of Aquilla, Texas, and I'm out here preparing my sermon for tomorrow morning."

"Why aren't all the other preachers out here at night? We've never seen anyone out here talking to himself before."

"I don't know about them, but this is what I'm supposed to be doing."

One of the boys said, "Preach, since you're here, I want to ask you a question I've wondered about for a long time."

"Great," I replied. "What's the question?" Inside I was saying, "Lord, help me not to blow this. It must be an important question."

He asked, "Which came first, God, the Stone Age, or man?"

"Well, here's the answer. Before you could name a rock, the rock had to be. It would be impossible to name something you've never seen or heard or thought of before. Rocks had to come before man. Then man named them. Obviously, God had to come before the rock, because God had to make the rock; the rock did not make itself."

The boy leaned forward and said, "You are the smartest man I have ever met in all my life." That established something about the intellectual level of my congregation!

The group was prepared, with full paraphernalia, for a rumble that night, but the other gang hadn't arrived yet. The leader of the gang said, "I want to know if I'll go to hell for saying this. . . ." He cursed foully, using vulgar words.

I replied, "The answer to your question is in the Bible. God says that a man speaks out of the abundance or overflow of his heart.[1] I would say, judging by what you've just said, that your heart is full of trash. The Bible also says that as a man thinks in his heart, so is he.[2] So, if you speak trash, it means your heart is full of trash." Looking intently into his eyes, I slowly said, "If your heart is full of trash, it means *you are trash!*"

I got his full attention!

The gang leader was furious. Just then a car squealed up to the curb. Seven boys piled out of the car fully prepared for a rumble. They started toward us.

I looked at the leader of "my" gang and said, "Go tell them to come over here and sit down. I want to talk to them."

"Preacher, if you know them that well, go tell them yourself."

"You do exactly what I tell you right now. Get up and go!"

He got up and went.

I heard him say, "Hey! You're not going to believe what I'm going to tell you. There's a real preach over there. It's the strangest thing you ever saw. He says he wants to talk to you."

All seven boys came over and sat down. My midnight congregation had more than doubled. Now twelve were sitting in a circle around me. The boys sat there and asked reasonably good questions for about half an hour—about Christ, God, eternity, heaven, hell. I told them the story of salvation.

When I felt I had said all that God wanted me to, I got up to leave and told them, "Now, men, this has been a miraculous night in your lives. God has sent one of His children to talk to you and tell you that He loves you."

During the next two nights, two of the twelve boys sought me out separately, wanting to hear again how to know God.

In an effort to follow up the decisions of these two young

---

[1]Luke 6:45
[2]Proverbs 22:7

men, I started a neighborhood weekly Bible study in their area, which resulted in the conversion and growth of other family members. One of these boys demonstrated a hunger to grow, and we spent months together in a Paul-Timothy relationship.

Principles to note:

1) God's leading in evangelism will not always seem logical. Frequently, the times and places for His harvest will come as a complete surprise to you. This means that *daily fellowship* and *yieldedness* to His leading are vitally important to the success of your personal ministry.

2) Because of the assurance that the Holy Spirit will guide your choice of words, you can *witness with boldness.* On many occasions, you will be as surprised at what you say or do as those with whom you're sharing.

Mrs. Tucker

A woman with an attractive little box was seated next to me. I watched her open it and take out her Bible and her Mary Baker Eddy book.

I said to her, "For you to have a Bible must mean that you are interested in Christ."

She replied, "Yes, I am a Christian Scientist. I've been one for twenty-two years. I'm about to do my daily readings."

"I've always wanted to talk to a devout Christian Scientist, because I would like to hear how you would share Christ with me from your background and perspective." So I asked her to pretend that I was a lost person and to witness to me from the training she had received. She happily agreed to do so.

She asked me about myself, then said, "Have you ever been seriously sick?"

"No, I never have."

"Are you whole?"

"Yes, I'm physically healthy. What I'd really like to know is how to go to heaven."

So she showed me numerous verses about physical illness.

I told her what I needed to know was how to go to heaven. I wanted to learn how to know God.

She tried for twenty minutes to witness to me. She couldn't locate a single clear verse on salvation. She had verses marked throughout her Bible, *but not one* dealt with salvation.

Finally, I said, "Mrs. Tucker, I'm frankly amazed and surprised that you haven't yet told me how to go to heaven."

She was utterly frustrated.

I said, "Now let's play the game the other way. As an evangelical Christian, I'll show you the way I'd tell someone how they can go to heaven. You pretend you're the lost person now."

I started by showing her the Bridge Illustration, beginning with Romans 3:23. After reading the verse, she said, "Now, of course, there is no such thing as sin."

I reminded her that she was now playing the part of a lost person and would, therefore, not have any predetermined interpretation of the Bible verses I was sharing. She politely agreed. Since I had listened to her for twenty minutes and had not given any interpretations to her verses, now it was her turn to do the same.

We went through the whole Bridge Illustration together. She said, "I've never seen this before, but it conflicts with what I have been taught and I cannot accept it."

"I understand your feelings, but let me encourage you to think more deeply," I replied. "The clear message of forgiveness and rebirth is found right here in God's Word. The real question is do you accept the Bible or not? You can't just believe little bits of its messages. Nowhere in the Scriptures does it say, 'Beware! Half the Bible isn't true'."

Healing is certainly a major emphasis in the Bible, but when Jesus restored the man who was sick of palsy and commanded him to take up his bed and walk, it was His more important words that amazed the unbelieving Pharisees: "Thy sins are forgiven thee."[3]

As we talked, it was immediately obvious that her spiritual

---

[3]Mark 2:9

eyes were starting to open. She was beginning to think about the centrality of Christ and the significance of His death on the Cross when He became our sin. ("For he hath made him to be sin for us, who knew no sin; that we might be made the righteousness of God in him" 2 Cor. 5:21.)

Principles to note:

1) One of the most meaningful ways to share the true message of Christ with friends who are sincerely religious but lost is to ask them to use their own Bible and *explain the plan of salvation* from its pages. Frequently they will discover their own lack of knowledge and understanding and will seek your help. Or it will come to their attention that they are interpreting the Scriptures in light of a secondary work, rather than letting the Bible speak for itself. This discovery will encourage them to read the Scriptures with a new desire to understand it under the Holy Spirit's guidance.

2) It is as important to *listen* in evangelism as it is to speak. We often have only a caricature of what other people believe, so it is important to prayerfully listen to their comments before attempting to share the message of God's love in Christ.

7

The Power for Witnessing Is a Person

Jesus said, "But you shall receive power when the Holy Spirit has come upon you; and you shall be My witnesses both in Jerusalem, and in all Judea and Samaria, and even to the remotest part of the earth" (Acts 1:8 NASB).

Now that this prophecy of the Lord has been fulfilled, when does a Christian receive power for witnessing? This is a question that should be dealt with early in a Timothy's training. The answer is simple—power for witnessing is given to every believer at conversion.

The powerful Person—God—enters a new convert's life through the baptism of the Holy Spirit the moment he acts on the decision to receive Christ as his Lord and Savior. "For we were *all* baptized by one *Spirit* into one *body*—whether Jews or Greeks, slave or free . . ." (1 Cor. 12:13). Becoming part of the Body of Christ is the result of the miracle called rebirth! On the foundation of a personal decision and this conversion experience, the new Christian grows and learns to live by faith on a day-to-day basis.

During this process, new and maturing believers should be carefully led to avoid making quests for new experiences. What they need is help in learning to continually grow in the fullness of Christ through time in God's Word, prayer, Scripture memory, and Christian fellowship. Satan is eager to sidetrack their newfound enthusiasm and commitment and may even use seemingly good or religious activities to accomplish his ends.

This is particularly true when believers sense an honest spiritual need in their lives and attempt to fill that need in a sincere but immature manner.

Our enemy is well aware of our ups and downs. The Book of Job indicates that Satan had a pretty good idea of where Job was spiritually, day by day. It should come as no surprise when he attempts to plant doubts in our minds during our weak moments.

With this understanding, it becomes important for us to ground our Timothys in good doctrine. They need to be led in a Bible study on the subject of the work and ministry of God the Spirit, so they will understand how a Christian is empowered for witnessing and godly living.

The Spirit-filled Life

In my own life as a young believer, while yearning to find some answers about the power of the Holy Spirit, I was given a book by Charles G. Finney, a well-known nineteenth-century author. He listed more than ninety things that an individual needed to do to be empowered and filled with the Holy Spirit.

Taking a day off to be alone with God, I went to the seclusion of a nearby Christian conference center and there prayed, "Father, what does it take? What is needed in my life for You to fill me with Your Spirit?" I proceeded through item 46 in the book. For several hours, I sought to get myself to the place where God could use me. After sincerely trying, I realized that I would never be able to juggle all ninety of those spiritual disciplines at the same time. In frustration, I just sat down on the floor and cried. There seemed to be no way that all the attitudes, character qualities, and spiritual attributes described by the author could go on simultaneously in my life. Though this saintly man was the greatest evangelist of his day, his otherwise excellent writings only succeeded in complicating my early understanding of the simplicity of the Spirit-filled life.

Several years later, I received a valuable insight from Bill Bright, the founder of Campus Crusade for Christ. His simple and understandable explanation of the Holy Spirit's ministry revolutionized the quality of my Christian life.

I discovered that the Christ-controlled, or Spirit-filled, life involves meeting only *three* scriptural conditions:

1) Being Born Again Spiritually

"Jesus answered, 'I tell you the truth, unless a man is born of water and the Spirit, he cannot enter the kingdom of God. Flesh gives birth to flesh, but the Spirit gives birth to spirit. You should not be surprised at my saying, 'You must be born again' " (John 3:5-7). Rebirth comes by believing in the claims and saving work of Jesus Christ to the degree that one willingly receives Him as Lord and Master. "Yet to all who *received* him, to those who *believed* in his name, he gave the right to become children of God" (John 1:12).

2) Being Clean Spiritually

A Christian must *consistently confess his sins* when they occur and maintain a clean heart before the Lord. "If we confess our sins, he is faithful and just and will forgive us our sins and purify us from all unrighteousness" (1 John 1:9).

3) Living by Faith

By faith, we must believe that we are filled by God's Spirit. This requires acting on the reality that being filled and controlled by the Holy Spirit is the normal way for Christians to live. The Bible says, "Understand what the Lord's will is . . . be filled with the Spirit. Speak to one another with psalms, hymns and spiritual songs. Sing and make music in your heart to the Lord, always giving thanks to God the Father for everything" (Eph. 5:17-20).

Being filled and controlled by the Holy Spirit is a sustained volitional decision of faith. It is not something we must wait for, nor can it be identified by a certain feeling. It is a chosen way of life.

Power Is Not a Feeling

On one mission trip overseas, I was healthy, and I preached with a strong physical awareness of God's power. Many committed themselves to Christ. The next time I preached in that

same country, I was physically ill and fatigued. I felt no awareness of power, yet as I bore witness to Christ, even larger
numbers responded to the gospel!

Nowhere does the Bible describe spiritual power as a feeling;
power is the work of a divine Person. That wonderful Person
is within you, both in times of sickness and in times of health.
He empowers, teaches, and convicts, based on His divine
promises in the Scriptures. Your simple willingness to give Him
complete control of your life is the key to useability. As one
sage has written, "Spiritual power comes from *trusting* rather
than from *trying.*"

Lead your Timothy to examine his heart and honestly confess his spiritual needs to God. Seek to deal with wrong attitudes, thoughts, and objectives that have grieved the Holy
Spirit and short-circuited the normal flow of spiritual power in
his life. After he confesses his sins to God, reexamine 1 John
1:9. Then lead him to begin *thanking* God that he is cleansed
from sin, restored to full fellowship, and filled with the Holy
Spirit. The *experience of power* comes hand in hand with the
understanding that the Holy Spirit's power is *continually present*
and *available* if His ministry is not quenched by our willful
disobedience.

Imagine for a minute that you have a sponge in your hand.
Squeeze the sponge tightly; now submerge it completely in a
bucket of water. At this moment, though the sponge is in the
water, very little water is in the sponge. It is only when you
release your grip that the sponge is filled.

In this same manner, your will can keep you from being
filled and controlled by God's Spirit. This possibility constantly
exists even though as a Christian you were baptized into His
body by His Spirit when you were born again.

The key to being filled with the Holy Spirit is not in having
another experience but simply in remaining yielded and totally
open to the will of God. Don't quench the working of God's
Spirit by attempting to rule and possess your own life. Lordship
means exactly what you might expect. Serving Christ best and
enjoying life most come when we experience continual yield-

edness to His perfect will. Spiritual power comes as the result of being filled, and being filled comes as the result of being controlled. Being controlled comes as the result of the moment-by-moment, day-by-day decision to be yielded.

Character Reveals Spiritual Power

I once had a private conference with a woman who was deeply confused[1] about the doctrine of the Holy Spirit. The focus of her faith was on the need for contemporary manifestations of signs, gifts, and miracles. Her recurring questions had plagued her for some seventeen years, and her confusion had taken her to such extremes that she had lost her close relationship with her parents. Her constant debating about doctrine had weakened her marriage and on one occasion had almost led to violence.

After a thorough Bible study on the person and work of the Holy Spirit, she was joyfully relieved from her anxiety. She had been relying on spiritual extremes and purely emotional experiences for fulfillment. She saw that her standard of spirituality was based on a misguided understanding of spiritual power.

As we talked, she asked sincerely, "If my answer is not in external signs and miracles or a second blessing, then where is the answer? Where is the power in the church today?"

I asked her whom she considered to be the world's most Spirit-filled and controlled man prior to the earthly ministry of the Lord Jesus Himself.

She replied, "I don't really know."

"Let me ask you this," I said. "If you discovered that the Bible taught that there was a man who was filled with the Holy Spirit even before his birth; whose life pleased God to such a degree that Jesus Himself would say, 'No greater man was ever born of a woman'; who had the Holy Spirit so dominant in his

---

[1]For full explanation, see Appendix 4.

life that Jesus applauded his ministry—would you consider such a man to be a good example of a powerful, Spirit-filled person?"

She replied, "Yes, if there were such a person, I believe I would."

I said, "Why don't we take a look at the Scriptures."

Together, we looked at the life of John the Baptist. We began by examining the testimony of John's contemporaries when they spoke to Jesus. "And many people came to him. They said, 'Though John never performed a miraculous sign, all that John said about this man was true' " (John 10:41).

John did not do any signs or perform any miracle in his entire ministry!

Next, we moved to the amazing prophecy about John. The angel of the Lord who appeared to his father, Zechariah, said, "He will be great in the sight of the Lord. He is never to take wine or other fermented drink, and he will be filled with the Holy Spirit even from birth" (Luke 1:15).

John the Baptist is the only man in the history of the world who was filled with the Holy Spirit from birth. He was the first and only one! God made an unusual exception in the person of John.

Isn't it interesting that a man indwelt by the Holy Spirit from birth never performed a miracle? He is the man of whom Jesus said, "I tell you the truth: Among those born of women there has not risen anyone greater than John the Baptist" (Matt. 11:11). By this, Jesus meant John was the greatest man ever born through natural birth. As a babe, Christ Himself was filled with the Holy Spirit without measure; however, He was born of a virgin, not through the natural human process.

Obviously, the secret of John's greatness was that he was indwelt and empowered by the Holy Spirit. Yet, in contrast to other prophets before him, he never performed a miracle. His ministry was so powerful that Jesus said of him, "And if you are willing to accept it, he is the Elijah who was to come" (Matt. 11:14).

A further passage we looked at was the angel's prediction of John's ministry. "And he will go on before the Lord, in the spirit and power of Elijah, to turn the hearts of the fathers to their children and the disobedient to the wisdom of the righteous—to make ready a people prepared for the Lord" (Luke 1:17).

It was Elijah who worked some of the more spectacular miracles in the Old Testament. He represents the kind of ministry typified by signs performed by God's miraculous power. John the Baptist came in the same Spirit and power, but the nature of his ministry was completely different.

What did John come to do? He came to point people toward the Messiah, Jesus Christ.[2] What was the evidence of the Spirit-filled power in John's life? It was the fact that his godly character and verbal witness got the attention of the whole nation and shook his generation.

Notice his results: "And in that place many believed in Jesus" (John 10:42). They believed in Jesus as a result of the witness of John without any miracle or signs.

What made John great in the sight of God? Certainly not his signs or his miracles: he did not perform any. God isn't impressed with miracles for the simple reason that He makes them all. What most impresses God is *faithfulness and obedience* to His mission. John was faithful and obedient for thirty-plus years. He did not suffer a moral lapse as did David, but lived a Spirit-controlled life. He pleased God.

His attitude was continually one of humility and Christ-centeredness. One day late in his ministry, his disciples came to him saying, " 'Rabbi, that man who was with you on the other side of the Jordan—the one you testified about—well, he is baptizing, and everyone is going to him!' To this John replied, 'A man can receive only what is given him from heaven. You yourselves can testify that I said, "I am not the Christ but am sent ahead of him" . . . He must become greater; I must become lesser' " (John 3:26-28, 30). When one views John the Baptist as the example of a powerful life that truly pleases God,

---

[2]See John 10:41; Luke 1:17

the emphasis is clearly placed on integrity, courage, character, and proclaiming the truth of the gospel.

Evangelism Reveals Spiritual Power

The Holy Spirit wants to use us to bear witness concerning Jesus Christ and to lift up and exalt Him today just as He did through John. The authentic power of the Holy Spirit is evidenced by the clear, authoritative testimony that "Jesus is Lord to the glory of God the Father" (Eph. 2:10-11). This is the supreme evidence of the power of the Holy Spirit.

The priority of witnessing is born out by Jesus' last words before the Ascension. "But you will receive power when the Holy Spirit comes on you; and you will be my witnesses in Jerusalem, and in all Judea and Samaria, and to the ends of the earth" (Acts 1:8). He did not say that we will do signs and miracles. The emphasis was on *bearing witness* to His divinity.

Evangelism is the evidence of an empowered life. If you are not reaching people with your testimony—with your verbal, personal witness as you go through life—it means that you have not chosen to "train yourself to be godly" (1 Tim. 4:7), and you have not yet given Him full control of your life.

The evidence of an empowered life is not the gifts of the Spirit, nor is it miracles. It's that your life is faithful and obedient to the mission God has given you (the Great Commission—Matt. 28:18-20), and that you are bearing faithful and effective witness to the *truth*.

Always remember that for every person who has been won to Christ because of a miracle, a million and probably many more have been brought to Jesus through a simple verbal witness.

You have lips—you can communicate. You have a hand—you can write a letter to a lost friend or loved one. You may say, "That seems so mundane." It wasn't mundane for John; that's what he lived for! You may say, "That's so unspectacular; you can't draw a crowd with that." When you speak the truth in the power of God, there will be people who will want to listen. In every generation, and seemingly even more so today, there are people who will respond to the truth.

The apostle Paul taught that God is sovereign. When He wants to use the gifts of the Spirit to perform miracles, He has the power to do so. And when He does, it will bring glory to Him! He carefully selects the time, the place, and the circumstances involved in using His gifts. In 1 Corinthians 12:11, Paul states that the Holy Spirit distributes His gifts to each one "just as He wills" (NASB).

It has been my observation that on those occasions when God has chosen to use one of His miraculous gifts, the individual through whom He worked was at first surprised, because the gift had not been deserved, nor had it been sought. It is my deep conviction that "seeking" and "tarrying" for power as related to the gifts is not only unnecessary but unbiblical.

On one memorable occasion before the rule of Idi Amin, I was visiting with Festo Kivengere, the beloved Anglican bishop and evangelist of Uganda. I asked, "Festo, why is it that in certain places, including Uganda, God has been able to bless His people with sustained revival?"

Bishop Kivengere gave a beautiful answer, "When God visited us with wonderful revival and periodically demonstrated His power through a miracle, the people did not presume that this meant that they were supposed to go into the miracle business. They were willing to let God do it once in their experience."

The key to evangelism is openness and integrity. To lust for power and attempt to manipulate or dominate God is the pitfall of many who seek power on their own terms. Carefully guard your Timothys from those who might lead them to seek power rather than the Person who is the power. Emphasize the fact that God never said that He would act at our beck and call. In fact, it is our objective as Christians to act at His beck and call. The Scriptures declare, "it is God who works in you to will and to act according to his good purpose" (Phil 2:13).

The Person is the power. To be controlled by Him is life's highest objective and greatest success. The Lord's brief span of humanity is our perfect example. He was the picture of weakness in terms of:

formal education,
financial resources,
family background,
political influence,
social status, and
official religious standing,

yet because He was totally yielded, filled, and obedient to the Person of the Holy Spirit, He was and is the single most powerful Person who ever lived. It is only *yieldedness* that makes us strong. In this little-understood reality, we are like our Lord. The same Holy Spirit who lived in Him lives in us as born-again believers today. He is our power!

8

Universal Joy!

The primary prerequisite for the Lord's return is the worldwide proclamation of the gospel. Therefore, it is our highest privilege as Christians to bear witness! The urgency of spreading His message was made clear as Jesus talked with His apostles on Mount Olivet: "And this gospel of the kingdom will be preached in the whole world as a testimony to all nations, and then the end will come" (Matt. 24:14).

Let the emphasis of Jesus' prophetic statement sink deeply into your heart. The people of every race and nation must learn about the meaning of Christ's first coming as the prerequisite for His second coming. Although we realize that not all will say yes, we can rejoice that countless millions will—regardless of their culture, group, or nationality. *The Good News is universal!*

The Good News was announced by an angel at Jesus' birth: "Do not be afraid. I bring you good news of *great joy* that will be for *all* people" (Luke 2:10). At a practical level, we want our Timothys to understand that this means God's Good News is neither Western nor Eastern—it is beyond culture. Christ alone enables an individual to know God personally! His sinless life, sacrificial death, and victorious resurrection have opened the door for God's love to make an impact on the lives of all people.

The world's most urgent need is to hear Christ's message, and *our* most urgent need is to deliver it! As we speak, our joy is made complete by the fact that at the last day there will be redeemed representatives of every group of humankind. We know this will occur, because the Bible says Jesus' sacrificial death purchased "men for God from every tribe and language and people and nation" (Rev. 5:9).

In Your Neighborhood

In today's neighborhoods, there are all kinds of people. It doesn't make any difference whether your next-door neighbor is an atheist, a Buddhist, a Muslim, or a Mormon—God loves them all. It is both your responsibility and privilege to share salvation in Jesus Christ with your neighbors under the leadership of the Holy Spirit.

Every Christian needs to equip himself or herself with a basic understanding of non-Christian religions. The ease of travel and the amazing speed of communication are making the world much smaller. It is therefore no longer just missionaries who must be able to converse easily with people of varied religious backgrounds.

For example, a friend of mine lives in a fairly typical neighborhood in his part of the United States. On his block he has Jewish, Hindu, Roman Catholic, and Protestant neighbors. Added to this, there are, or course, various types of secularists who worship "the good life" and material possessions. Close by, there are new buildings representing two growing North American cults, so some of his neighbors are probably Mormons or Jehovah's Witnesses.

All of this is to say that we need to become sensitive to those around us. Too many of us reach out only to people who are most like ourselves. We have made no provision to witness to those of other backgrounds.

Peter stated, "But in your hearts set apart Christ as Lord. Always be prepared to give an answer to everyone who asks you to give the reason for the hope that you have" (1 Peter 3:15). And "everyone" means "everyone"!

A Spiritual Family

We must be sure that each Timothy learns to see himself as a participant in the world at large, not just in one little pocket or province. As a born-again Christian, he is not just a North American or a South American, an Asian, a European, or a Middle Easterner. He is a citizen of the kingdom of God.

Every time you lead someone to a saving knowledge of Jesus Christ, the kingdom of God has been extended—by one. After that, his real identity is no longer determined by his nationality or ethnic origin. He owes his undivided allegiance to Jesus Christ as his King, his Lord, and his Master.

This perspective is important for evangelism. If a new Christian does not understand that God's objective is to have a worldwide spiritual family, his understanding of outreach can be extremely provincial and limited.

Back in seminary days, while I was preaching on weekends, a fellow seminarian asked me, "Billie, how were your evangelistic services?"

I enthusiastically replied, "The kingdom of God was extended by several people this week."

He looked at me with a puzzled expression on his face. He had not yet learned to think of evangelism in terms of God's kingdom, but was used to discussing the number of converts in a crusade.

When a person is born again, he does not just become a member of his denomination or local fellowship, as important as that may be. He becomes part of an everlasting family, an eternal spiritual kingdom.

The Process of Evangelism

Evangelism is normal in a healthy Christian life. It is a *process* more than a *program*.

When we disciple our Timothys, we must teach them theology as well as methodology. The two must be carefully balanced. In training them in evangelism, we must not only show them *how* to lead someone to Christ but also tell them *why* they should evangelize. If our Timothys do not understand the importance of the *why,* they may witness for a few years, but evangelism will never become an enduring part of their lifestyle.

When I was a small boy and had just become a Christian myself, I did not know the plan of salvation well enough to explain it to someone else—but I did know Jesus Christ personally. So I shared my testimony with a close friend who was ten years old. I told him my story of conversion, and to my knowledge that was the beginning of his serious interest in Christ. Soon he received Jesus as his Savior, too. I didn't know a single verse to share with him, but I had met the Person whom he needed to know. That introduction is the beginning place for evangelism. We are not merely sharing facts, but a living Person.

As I matured and entered my teens, I learned a few verses from the Book of Romans that helped me explain how someone could come to know Jesus Christ personally (Rom. 3:23; 6:23; 5:8; and 10:9-10). This gave me a sense of confidence and made me a little more skillful in evangelism—and the process continued.

Later, in college, I learned the Bridge Illustration, which enabled me to put the gospel on paper and demonstrate it pictorially. It was a simple but effective tool that God used to lead a number of my friends to Christ.

From that point forward, with the basic foundation laid, I was able to devote my time to selecting key verses and illustrations for personally sharing Christ with an ever-expanding group of people. Over the years, there has been no time for boredom in terms of evangelism, because there are always new individuals with new needs. Though our message never really changes, like Paul on Mars Hill, we must find fresh ways to communicate the truth of Christ to people from every conceivable background.

Now you might ask, "Do I need to teach comparative religion to my Timothy?"

No, not in the formal sense of the word. But you do need to explain why a contemporary Jewish person is typically expected to find difficulty in receiving Jesus as his Messiah (see chap. 9). He also needs to understand why a follower of Islam will normally have initial difficulty accepting the truth that Jesus Christ is God (see chap. 11).

Thinking of a Muslim, you might ask, "How on earth will I ever be able to talk about Christ with a person like that?"

Actually, it's not as difficult as you might think. When you boil it all down, the process begins with one biblical concept— God as Father. As this truth is shared from Scriptures, the convicting power of the Holy Spirit will begin to work in a person's heart.

God As "Father"

Before my first preaching experience in India, I asked a friend who had lived there how to share Christ with a Muslim. He replied, "Billie, don't begin with Romans 3:23. A better place to start is John 14:6: 'I am the way and the truth and the life. No one comes to the Father except through me.' "

You may ask, "Why start here?" The logic behind this is simple. A Muslim's background does not include a Christian understanding of God as Father. Therefore, you might begin something like this: "Jesus was speaking in the first person in the Holy Scriptures when He said, 'I am the way and the truth and the life. No one comes to the *Father* except through me.' "

The word Jesus uses here is *Abba* which means "Father." You would need to explain to your Muslim friend that the word, *Abba,* is an affectionate, personal word that literally means "Daddy." This will probably surprise him at first, because his religious training would never allow him the privilege of calling Allah his "Father."

Point out the fact that Jesus did *not* say, "I am the way and the truth and the life. No one comes to *God* except through me." Jesus could have easily chosen an Aramaic word that meant "God," but he carefully selected the word, "Abba." Why did He do that?

Let's visualize an evangelistic situation in which I am witnessing to a Muslim friend. I would say, "Akbar, why do you suppose Jesus used the word, 'Father,' here, instead of 'God'?"

Akbar would reply, "I'm not sure."

I would then say, "The answer to this question is very interesting. Every person will stand before God when he dies. The Bible teaches, 'Man is destined to die once, and after that to face judgment' (Heb. 9:27). Akbar, you already believe in the Judgment, don't you?"

"Yes, I do."

"All right. Jesus taught that when you die you will meet God in one of two ways: either you will meet Him as your *Father*, or you will stand before Him as your *Judge*.

"Akbar, the central message of the entire Bible is that God loves you and wants to be your Father, but it is also true that He will not be your Father or give you a place in heaven because of the sins you have committed. This is why God chose to come from heaven and die for you and me on the cross. At that moment, He took our judgment on Himself, paying for our sin and making it possible for us to know Him as our Father.

"Let me show you the verse that most clearly explains this important truth. Romans 5:8 says, 'But God demonstrates his own love for us in this: While we were still sinners, Christ died for us.' Sin must be paid for, but because of Christ we have a wonderful choice. We can accept the gift of forgiveness that Jesus Christ made possible when He died in our place, rather than choosing to meet God as our Judge and pay for our own sins throughout eternity.

"It was not ego or a sense of religious exclusivism but the reality of sin's penalty that made it necessary for Him to say, 'No one can come to the *Father* except through me.' "

After proceeding this far in the conversation, I would then ask the Holy Spirit to simply guide the remainder of our discussion; I would seek to faithfully present Christ and answer one question at a time. My prayer would be that Akbar would soon see that standing before God face to face outside of forgiveness in Christ is the most awesome and fearful experience a person can have.

Ironically, those who assert that they can meet God on their own terms are correct. They will meet Him, but they will immediately wish they hadn't. Tragically, rather than knowing Him as a kind, loving, and compassionate Father, they will meet Him as a righteous and impartial Judge. The full force of His wrath will be leveled at their sin on the basis that Jesus described in John 3:17-18: "For God did not send the Son into the world to judge the world; but that the world should be saved through Him. He who believes in Him is not judged; he who does *not* believe has been judged already, because he has *not* believed in the name of the only begotten Son of God" (NASB).

The objective of evangelism is to lead the people of all nations to wisely answer this question: "Do I choose to meet God as my Judge, or do I choose to meet Him as my Father?" The reason Jesus Christ came to earth was to enable men to know God in a totally new and different way—*To know Him* as their own heavenly Father.

Cultural Barrier

Beyond understanding theological needs, we must also be sensitive to cultural barriers that could complicate our witness. For many there will be estrangement from family, friends, and possibly even their homeland.

On one of my trips to India, a young Hindu man woke me early one morning. When I opened the door, he asked, "Can you convert me?"

I replied, "No, I don't have that power; but I do know Someone who does. If you'd like, I can introduce you to Him."

"Please do," he said.

I told him the only Person who had that power was God, and that He had revealed Himself to men as Jesus Christ of Nazareth. For the next half hour, I shared Christ with him from the Bible.

Before long, he said, "I want to become a Christian."

"Wait," I warned. "Are you sure you really do? If you accept Christ you will lose your job and be cast out by your family.

It will cost you everything you have in this world! You must be absolutely sure you really want to accept Christ."

Tears came to his eyes. He said, "For nearly two years I have been studying, and I have come to the conclusion that Jesus was who He claimed to be. This is why I have sought someone who could tell me how to be converted."

I said, "Are you telling me that you believe that Jesus is God in the very flesh? And that He is the only Savior?"

He replied, "I believe that, and I have no other option than to make Him my Lord."

I said, "That's true—you have no other option."

So we prayed together, and he received Christ. Immediately, I saw a change in his countenance. A new radiance and joy entered his personality. His search had ended!

In order to prepare him to explain his important decision, I told him not to tell anyone about his experience for seven days. During that time, we would meet each night for Bible study and prayer. He happily agreed.

The next afternoon, he was outside my door again, but he didn't look very happy. He said, "I must ask your forgiveness. I have not obeyed you."

I asked, "What did you do?"

He replied, "I told a friend. He's hiding around that corner. He wants to know Jesus, too!"

The cost related to identifying himself as a Christian could not keep him from sharing his new-found joy.

Though this happened in India, it could happen anywhere. For this reason, we must be prepared to introduce such people to Christ and then to enable them to adequately explain the *reason* for their new-found joy. If they are rejected, we must also become their new family; but in every case we must help them grow and must be their friend.

Christ is cross-cultural. He is the best news the world has ever had. Because of this, we must become equipped to effectively share His message—with all people.

9

The Key to Openness
With Jewish Friends

Although in the past it was generally considered difficult for
Christians to discuss the Messiah with Jewish friends and neighbors, that is not universally true today.

Once while flying to Philadelphia, I discovered that I was
seated next to an intelligent middle-aged Jewish lady. When
we made connections in Washington to go on to Los Angeles,
we were again assigned seats next to one another. That morning I had prayed for the opportunity to share Christ, so I sus-
pected this to be the Lord's answer. On the first leg of our trip,
I had discovered that she was a professor in an eastern college
and was en route to California to interview for a new university
position.

We had enjoyed casual conversation, so as our flight re-
sumed, I said, "I very seldom have the opportunity to talk with
a Jewish person in an unhurried situation like this. There's a
question I've been wanting to discuss for some time."

She seemed to genuinely appreciate my interest.

Five Levels of Judaism

I told her I had concluded that there were five different levels
of Judaism, and I wanted to know if my observation was correct.

She wondered what I meant by the word "levels," so I
explained.

1. *The Religious Level*—Many Jewish people, both in Israel
and throughout the rest of the world, are devout. They are

Jewish in religious affiliation and conviction. They have faith in Jehovah, the God of the Bible, and they practice their faith diligently.

2. *The Cultural Level*—Some are Jews culturally. They participate in their local Jewish community center, are involved in trying to preserve the Hebrew language and traditions, and are active in Jewish and Israeli affairs locally and worldwide. But they *do not* have a vital faith in the God of Israel.

3. *The Social Level*—Some are only Jewish socially; that is to say, many of their best friends and their business partners are still Jewish, but they have accepted the values and lifestyle of their communities so that they have all but lost their religious and cultural ties with the past.

4. *The Genealogical Level*—Some are Jewish only in terms of genealogy. They are members of the Jewish race because of their parents' ancestry. For them, being Jewish is simply like being a member of the Anglo-Saxon or any other race. Because one's race does not dictate a religious preference, it is therefore not unusual to find Jewish Christians in many parts of the world.

5. *The Nationality Level*—Some are Jewish by nationality. This means that they live in Israel and have Israeli citizenship. Their participation in religious affairs may, however, vary all the way from religious orthodoxy to atheism.

Jane readily agreed with the basic description of each level and suggested that her parents were at level one, her mother-in-law and father-in-law at level two, and she and her husband at level three. It was helpful to learn that she saw herself as Jewish only at a social level.

The majority of modern-day Jewish people whom I have met express few deep religious convictions. This is particularly true in the western world. Although they may strictly keep their traditional holidays and participate in their traditional cultural activities, only a small percentage are Jewish in terms of Old Testament faith (level 1). The average Jewish person is as open to the message of God's love as anyone, once he sees that Christianity is not a Gentile faith.

The Annas and Caiaphas Question

After I briefly explored the five levels with my new friend, I moved on to a second question, one that led to a positive discussion and enabled me to share from the Scriptures:

"Jane, I appreciate the fact that you have answered so honestly. As a Gentile, I have still another question. I would like to find out what it is that the Jewish community knows about Annas and Caiaphas that the Gentile community does not understand. Obviously you must have some deep insights into the character and teaching of these two men that we do not have."

Jane replied, "Who are Annas and Caiaphas?"

"They may well be the two most *significant* men in the last twenty centuries of Jewish life," I told her.

Puzzled, she said, "I've never heard of them."

"I am surprised you don't know a great deal about them. Most Jews follow them even today."

"They may be Jewish leaders," Jane replied, "but I still don't know who they are."

I said, "That's the whole point. This baffles us as Gentiles! Jane, let me put it into perspective. Here's the situation: History records that 2000 years ago there were four prominent figures in Israel's religious life. One of them was John the Baptist, one was Jesus of Nazareth, one was Annas, and one was Caiaphas. All four of them were nationally-known Jewish leaders." I went on to explain something about each of the four men.

John the Baptist was the son of a respected Jewish priest named Zacharias. John was the popular prophet of whom Jesus said no greater man has ever been born of woman. He was unique in Hebrew history, because he was the only prophet who ever had the Holy Spirit in his life from his mother's womb (see Luke 1:15). Hundreds and probably thousands of John's contemporaries flocked to hear him preach his powerful messages on personal purity and repentance. His theme was, "Repent, for the kingdom of God is at hand." It was he who prophesied at the River Jordan that Jesus of Nazareth was the promised Messiah—the Lamb of God, who would take away the sin of the world (John 1:29).

Jesus, whom they called Immanuel, was unique in almost every respect. His birth was announced by angels (Luke 1:26-35; 2:8-14). He was born *miraculously* to a devout Jewish virgin.[1] He lived a sinless life,[2] performed many miraculous signs,[3] came to die as man's sacrificial sinbearer,[4] rose victoriously from the grave,[5] taught His faithful Hebrew disciples,[6] and finally ascended to heaven[7] after appearing to more than 500 Jewish witnesses.[8] He clearly claimed to be the expected Messiah,[9] and without question remains the greatest Jew who has ever lived, for no man has ever affected the world as He has.

In addition, you have Annas and Caiaphas, who were the contemporary institutional leaders of the Jewish faith. Although neither man represented the lineage of the Levitical

---

[1]Matthew 1:18: "Now the birth of Jesus Christ was as follows. When His mother Mary had been betrothed to Joseph, before they came together she was found to be with child by the Holy Spirit" (NASB).

[2]2 Corinthians 5:21: "He made Him who knew no sin to be sin on our behalf, that we might become the righteousness of God in Him" (NASB).

[3]John 11:47: "Therefore the chief priests and the Pharisees convened a council, and were saying, 'What are we doing? For this man is performing many signs' " (NASB).

[4]1 Peter 2:24a: "and He Himself bore our sins in His body on the cross" (NASB).

[5]Matthew 28:5-6: "And the angel answered and said to the women, 'Do not be afraid; for I know that you are looking for Jesus who has been crucified. He is not here, for He has risen, just as He said. Come, see the place where He was lying' " (NASB).

[6]Acts 1:3: "To these He also presented Himself alive, after His suffering, by many convincing proofs, appearing to them over a period of forty days, and speaking of the things concerning the kingdom of God" (NASB).

[7]Acts 1:9: "And after He had said these things, He was lifted up while they were looking on, and a cloud received Him out of their sight" (NASB).

[8]1 Corinthians 15:6: "After that He appeared to more than five hundred brethren at one time, most of whom remain until now, but some have fallen asleep" (NASB).

[9]John 4:25-26: "The woman said to Him, 'I know that Messiah is coming (He who is called Christ); when that One comes, He will declare all things to us.' Jesus said to her, 'I who speak to you am He' " (NASB).

priesthood of the Old Testament, both had been appointed to serve in the position of high priest. They greatly influenced Judaism, both in Palestine and abroad. Historically, it was these two men who led the religious ruling body of 70, called the Sanhedrin, to declare that John the Baptist was not a legitimate prophet and that he was mistaken in his claims that Jesus was the expected Messiah. They took the position that Jesus was a blasphemer,[10] that He was demon possessed,[11] and that He was a deceiver.[12] They therefore believed that the testimony of His sinless life,[13] guiltless crucifixion,[14] and miraculous[15] resurrection[16] was not from God. They declared adamantly that the Messiah had not yet come.

From that day forward, the whole world has been forced into

---

[10]John 10:32-33: "Jesus answered them, 'I showed you many good works from the Father; for which of them are you stoning Me?' The Jews answered Him, 'For a good work we do not stone You, but for blasphemy; and because You, being a man, make Yourself out to be God' " (NASB).

[11]John 8:48: "The Jews answered and said to Him, 'Do we not say rightly that You are a Samaritan and have a demon?' " (NASB).

[12]Matthew 27:62-63: "Now on the next day, which is the one after the preparation, the chief priests and the Pharisees gathered together with Pilate, and said, 'Sir, we remember that when He was still alive that deceiver said, "After three days I am to rise again" ' " (NASB).

[13]Hebrews 4:15: "For we do not have a high priest who cannot sympathize with our weaknesses, but One who has been tempted in all things as we are, yet without sin" (NASB).

[14]Luke 23:13-14: "And Pilate summoned the chief priests and the rulers and the people, and said to them, 'You brought this man to me as one who incites the people to rebellion, and behold, having examined Him before you, I have found no guilt in this man regarding the charges which you make against Him' " (NASB).

[15]John 10:24-25: "The Jews therefore gathered around Him, and were saying to Him, 'How long will You keep us in suspense? If You are the Christ, tell us plainly.' Jesus answered them, 'I told you, and you do not believe; the works that I do in My Father's name, these bear witness of Me' " (NASB).

[16]John 10:17-18: "For this reason the Father loves Me, because I lay down My life that I may take it again. No one has taken it away from Me, but I lay it down on My own initiative. I have authorityy to lay it down, and I have authority to take it up again. This commandment I received from My Father" (NASB).

the position of determining which pair of these four men to believe. Should we trust in the integrity, morality, and judgment of Caiaphas and Annas, or should we trust in the integrity, morality, and testimony of John and Jesus? One set of Jewish leaders was right, and the other was wrong. Every Gentile in the world is risking his or her life and eternal destiny on the correctness of one Jew or the other.

Every Jewish person in the world who has not accepted Jesus as Messiah because Caiaphas and Annas said He was an imposter is risking his life, his eternal future, and ultimately his children's lives on the judgment and integrity of these two men.

These two men are faithfully followed by all Orthodox Jewish people today. Their universal influence has become the *primary reason* why people at all levels of Judaism have forfeited receiving Christ as their Savior. Why, then, are these men not among the best-known persons in Jewish religious life? Throughout the world, this remains a total mystery to students of Hebrew history.

If Annas and Caiaphas were right about Jesus, then all the miracles performed in the name of Christ[17] during the last twenty centuries have been psychological or demonic in origin. The life-changing events experienced by millions of Jews and Gentiles when they received Him as Savior[18] and Lord have all been false. Therefore, it is critically important for Jews and Gentiles alike to know everything possible about the morality, integrity, and spiritual qualities of Annas and Caiaphas. Whose lives did they change? Whom did they heal? What did they

---

[17]Acts 3:2, 6: "And a certain man who had been lame from his mother's womb was being carried along, whom they used to set down every day at the gate of the temple which is called Beautiful, in order to beg alms of those who were entering the temple . . . But Peter said, 'I do not possess silver and gold, but what I do have I give to you: In the name of Jesus Christ the Nazarene—walk!' " (NASB).

[18]Matthew 1:21: "And she will bear a Son; and you shall call His name Jesus, for it is He who will save His people from their sins" (NASB).

teach that has stood the test of time? What evidence do we have that God's anointing rested upon their lives? These are important questions that demand honest answers.

A New Perspective

After I had finished this brief explanation, Jane looked at me in amazement and said, "I have never thought about it like this before."

"Well, Jane, you need to, because everything in human history hinges on it. Your life, eternity, and the very purpose of your existence are determined by your decision on this issue. So I would strongly suggest that you ask a rabbi what he knows about Annas and Caiaphas.

"At my suggestion, a friend of mine recently did this. He talked with one of the leading rabbis in Texas and asked his opinion of Annas and Caiaphas."

After a brief pause, Jane asked, "Well, what did the rabbi say? Did he know who Annas and Caiaphas were?"

"Yes. He knew exactly who they were. To my friend's surprise, he replied immediately, saying that Annas and Caiaphas were the worst examples of priesthood that Judaism has ever produced. But for some reason, the rabbi failed to comprehend the significance of his statement. If he honestly had such a negative evaluation of these two important historical figures, why would he accept *their assessment* of John and Jesus, when the world recognizes them as the godliest of Jews?

"Jane, in your own research seek to find out why most Jewish people have followed these two little-known and apparently politically-motivated men for nearly twenty centuries. I have never met a Jewish person yet who can give me any additional information on Annas and Caiaphas that would substantiate the fact that they were godly, credible men worth believing. Yet they have been trusted and followed by countless thousands and millions of Jews across the centuries.

"As an outsider looking in, I have difficulty understanding how any Jewish person would find it undesirable to accept Jesus as his or her Messiah. My family are Gentiles, so when I worship a Jew, my wife worships a Jew, and my children worship a Jew, it is perplexing to see the preponderance of Jewish people following two other Jews.

"Ultimately I, like all men, had to take one Jewish position or the other; and based on the evidence, it was intellectually impossible for me to choose Annas and Caiaphas in preference to Jesus Christ. It seems ironic that if Caiaphas and Annas had led the Sanhedrin to *accept* Jesus as the expected Messiah, then all devout Jews would today be Christian, and all devout Christians would be Jews."

Summary and Conclusion

From this point, pursue the conversation as the Holy Spirit leads you. I have done this several times. The first Jewish person I ever led to Christ responded to this simple presentation. Up to that time, he had never seen the reality that his spiritual decision was not between Gentile faith and Jewish faith, but between two Jewish expressions of faith. Alleviating this misconception opened the door for his rebirth through faith in Jesus Christ as the Messiah.

There is nothing Gentile about Christianity! Christianity is uniquely, totally, and completely rooted in Judaism. Not one apostle was a Gentile, and few Gentiles were among the leaders of the early church. What everyone faces—Jew and Gentile alike—is making the decision as to which Jews had the truth from God.

Remember that this presentation is not the plan of salvation. This is only sharing a segment of truth that is helpful to a select group of people. It might be called, "pre-evangelism." After a Jewish person understands this line of reasoning, the Holy Spirit will quicken his desire to know more about the Jew, Jesus Christ.

Most Jewish friends who are ready to listen to the plan of salvation will receive Christ simply through the presentation of the Bridge Illustration. The majority of them have never clearly understood the gospel, even though it was first proclaimed for their own spiritual benefit.

In summary, the four things I would teach my Timothy to do in talking with a Jewish friend or acquaintance are:

1. Share the five levels of Judaism to find out how he sees himself.

2. Find out if he understands why he and his people have rejected John and Jesus in preference to following Annas and Caiaphas.

3. Affirm the fact that this decision has absolutely nothing to do with a Gentile faith but is strictly a personal and all-important response to an internal Jewish question.

4. Share your testimony and the Bridge Illustration. Explain to your Jewish friend what Jesus did as the Messiah and emphasize the truth of Jesus' statement, "I am the way and the truth and the life. No one comes to the Father except through me" (John 14:6).

10

Presenting the Trinity in Evangelism

In today's world, church members need to be especially well prepared to explain Christianity's most important doctrine—the Trinity. This is true because most cults are based on a distortion of this doctrine. Satan's first line of attack is to confuse and mislead both nonbelievers and Christians who are uninformed on this subject. In some instances, explaining the Trinity may need to be the first step in presenting the gospel.

This basic knowledge is important not only for witnessing to members of non-Trinitarian cults, but also for sharing Christ with followers of world religions. Both Roman Catholic and Protestant theologians have agreed on the teaching of this doctrine for many centuries. Most Protestant denominations unite together on this teaching, even though they may differ on less essential points of New Testament belief and practice. For the rest of your Timothy's life, he will be helped by this foundational knowledge as he bears his witness for our Lord.

Several years ago, after a conversation with a Jehovah's Witness, I realized my own need to be able to more fully demonstrate this great truth from the Bible. Some time after that, while on an overseas journey, I was privileged to sit next to Ron Carlson, a noted Swedish Baptist evangelist who speaks widely on the subject of leading non-Trinitarians to salvation. During our time together, I learned numerous important verses that have greatly helped me in showing people how to know and understand God.

As a non-Trinitarian thinks about these passages, the Holy Spirit will use them to convict him of the fact that the Trinity is the revealed nature of God. The following statement of purpose is a good place to begin:

If there is *one* God, and if there are *three Persons* called God in the Bible, then *by faith* I must accept the doctrine of the Trinity, even though I may not fully *comprehend* how God can be one yet three in perfect unity and equality at the same time.

In a discussion, this statement of purpose allows a non-Trinitarian to clearly understand what you are preparing to show him from the Bible. If he responds with openness, begin by showing him the divinity of Christ.

Understanding Jehovah

On one memorable occasion, while visiting the island of Cyprus, I met a man selling ice cream on the beach a short distance from my hotel. I noticed he had a Greek Bible on his ice cream stand.

I said to him, "You must be a believer—a Christian. I see that you have a Bible."

He smiled and replied, "I am a Jehovah's Witness Christian."

Although I knew his statement was not right, I simply said, "It's good to meet you. I am a Baptist Christian."

"I've never heard of a Baptist Christian. What do you believe?"

"We believe that Jesus is God."

He reacted with amazement. "Oh, no! That is not true!"

"Hasn't anyone ever shown you that from the Bible?" I asked.

"No, because it isn't true."

"Your Bible is in Greek," I said. "Mine is in English. Why don't we compare the verses on the subject and see if they agree?"

He told me that he'd been a Greek Orthodox for many years but had never been taught much about how to know Christ. Then fifteen years before, some Jehovah's Witnesses had invited him to a Bible study. Because of a real hunger for the Scriptures, he responded to their invitation and ultimately became a Jehovah's Witness.

I went to my room and got my Bible. Then I wrote the statement of purpose (page 132) at the top of a piece of paper, followed by seven brief verses of Scripture. These alone would be enough to demonstrate the first part of the statement of purpose.

When I got back to the ice cream stand, three Jehovah's Witnesses were waiting for me. One of them was a missionary from England who was curious to hear what I was going to say. I explained that I would show them from the Scriptures that Jesus is God. They were skeptical, but interested.

I said, "*If* I can show you that there are three Persons called God in the Bible, yet one God, then by faith you'll have to accept the Trinity (statement of purpose), won't you?"

With some consternation, they agreed and asked me to go through those passages with them.

(When sharing these Scriptures with a non-Trinitarian, use a cover sheet and don't allow him to see all the references at once. Discuss one verse at a time. Too often, he is not nearly so committed to listening and really thinking as he is to simply winning an argument. As you go over the passages one by one, pray that the truth of each verse will make its full impact on his heart.)

As I expected, my three new friends kept trying to leave these verses and pursue various tangents. I continually brought them back to the outline with this promise: "After we look at these seven passages, I will be very happy to discuss any other verses that are on your mind. However, if you don't let me thoroughly finish going over these seven, I'll leave." Then, with a smile, I surprised them by saying, "And if I leave, you may never learn the truth!"

Because of the language barrier, it took us about two hours (normally, in one language, twenty to thirty minutes would be adequate):

There Is One God

1. We began with Deuteronomy 6:4—"Hear, O Israel: The LORD our God, the LORD is one." I said, "There is only one God." They readily agreed.

2. We continued with Isaiah 43:10-11—" 'You are my witnesses,' declares the LORD, 'and my servant whom I have chosen, so that you may know and believe me and understand that I am He. Before me no god was formed, nor will there be one after me. I, even I, am the LORD, and apart from me there is no savior.' " At this point, I made some observations:

—God is speaking here in the first person.

—He says there has been no god before Him and will be none after Him. God is not a liar, so when He says this, you know it must be true.

—He is the LORD and only Savior.

Again, they immediately agreed.

3. We then looked at Isaiah 44:6—"This is what the LORD says—Israel's King and Redeemer, the LORD Almighty: I am the first and I am the last; apart from me there is no God." I emphasized the fact that God is speaking *in the first person*. Our one God, Jehovah (the LORD), says, "I am the *first* and I am the *last.*"

Before going further, I briefly reviewed these first three passages again, for they clearly established the first part of the statement of purpose ("there is one God"). The Bible clearly affirms monotheism. He is One, and He is the first and the last—the only God. Up to this point, my hearers were quite pleased to agree with me.

Jesus Is God

4. Next, we read Revelation 1:8—" 'I am the Alpha and the Omega,' says the Lord God, 'who is, and who was, and who is to come, the Almighty.' " I made some more observations:

—Jehovah (the Almighty) is speaking in the first person.

—He says He is the Alpha and the Omega.

—He says He is, He was, and that He is to come.

5. Then we turned to Revelation 22:13 and found the same God speaking again—"I am the Alpha and the Omega, the First and the Last, the Beginning and the End." The description, "I am *the first* and I am *the last,*" from Isaiah 44:6, clearly unifies the Old Testament and New Testament identity of Jehovah God. At this point, I asked the following questions:

—Who is "The first and the last, the only Savior"?

—Who is speaking in the first person in this passage?

The answer is in Revelation 22:16—"I, *Jesus,* have sent my angel to give you this testimony for the churches."

As the three men wrestled with these questions and the answer, I carefully explained, "The same Jehovah, who was the first and the last in the Old Testament, now speaks in the New Testament and calls Himself the first and the last. This time, it is Jesus who is speaking! Therefore, Jesus and Jehovah are that one, *same,* God, who is, who was, and who is to come, the Almighty."

Next, we turned back to Revelation 1:1—"The revelation of Jesus Christ . . . ." This made it clear that Jesus is the One speaking in this book. He is the author of the Book of Revelation, the first and the last, the beginning and the end. He is the Lord God Almighty (Rev. 1:8). He is the only LORD and Redeemer of Isaiah 44:6. He is the only God of Isaiah 43:10-11. Jesus clearly identifies Himself as God.

6. After a brief discussion, we turned to Revelation 1:17-18: "When I saw him, I fell at his feet as though dead. Then he placed his right hand on me and said: 'Do not be afraid. I am the First and the Last. I am the Living One; I was dead, and behold I am alive for ever and ever! And I hold the keys to death and Hades.' " These thoughts were emphasized:

—Again, God is speaking in the first person.

—When did God ever die? When did the first and the last ever die and rise again?

—Jesus is the only One who ever died and rose again. Therefore, He is God; He is Jehovah.

7. Finally, we turned to Hebrews 1:7-8—"In speaking of the angels he says, 'He makes His angels winds, his servants

flames of fire.' But about the *Son* he says, 'Your throne, O God, will last for ever and ever, and righteousness will be the scepter of your kingdom.' "

—In this verse, God the Father calls the Son—GOD!

—Who could better understand who God is than God Himself?

In summary, God the Father has clearly said that Jesus is God in Hebrews 1. He has credited Him as being the Creator of the world (v. 2), the radiance of His glory (v. 3), the exact representation of His nature, and exercising the power by which all that exists is being upheld (v. 4).

The Holy Spirit Is God

After training our Timothys to demonstrate that Jesus is God from the Scriptures, we must then show them how to prove that the Holy Spirit is God, too. Until this important fact has been established from the Scriptures, the original proposition (see pages 121-122) will be incomplete.

Groups such as the Jehovah's Witnesses lower God the Holy Spirit to the position of being an impersonal force or an "it." Non-Christian monotheists believe in one god, but they do not accept Him as a trinity. This not only means that they usually reject the biblical claim of the divinity of Christ, but that they also reject the divinity of the Holy Spirit. To reject either is, in reality, to reject all! Romans 8:9 is a good example of this basic truth: "However you are not in the flesh but in the Spirit, if indeed the Spirit of God dwells in you. But if anyone does not have the Spirit of Christ, he does not belong to Him" (NASB). Paul equates the Spirit of God with the Spirit of Christ! The Holy Spirit may be called by either name, but He must live in you if you are to be a born-again child of God—a Christian. To deny the person of the Holy Spirit is to reject the person of Christ, and vice versa.

A number of passages clearly demonstrate the Holy Spirit's personhood and deity.

1. "*God is Spirit,*" (John 4:24) To see this truth, we can begin with Acts 5:1-4—"Now a man named Ananias, together

with his wife Sapphira, also sold a piece of property. With his wife's full knowledge he kept back part of the money for himself, but brought the rest and put it at the apostles' feet.

"Then Peter said, 'Ananias, how is it that Satan has so filled your heart that you have *lied to the Holy Spirit* and have kept for yourself some of the money you received for the land? Didn't it belong to you before it was sold? And after it was sold, wasn't the money at your disposal? What made you think of doing such a thing? You have *not lied to men but to God*.' "

This incident made it graphically clear to the early Christian community that to lie to the Holy Spirit was to lie to God. Peter fully *equated* the Holy Spirit with the person of God Himself.

2. *God the Spirit is personal and knowable.* Move to Acts 13:1-3—"In the church at Antioch there were prophets and teachers . . . worshiping the Lord and fasting . . . the *Holy Spirit said*, 'Set apart for me Barnabas and Saul for the work to which *I have called them*.' So after they had fasted and prayed, they placed their hands on them and sent them off."

Stop and think. Is it possible for an impersonal "it" or force to call someone or to speak to anyone in this way? The Book of Acts derives its name from the acts of a divine person whom Jesus called the Helper—the Holy Spirit. It was He who empowered, guided, and taught the apostles and all the other believers in the early church. He is the One who inspired Luke to write his letter in this specific way.

Note that the message is given in the first person, "I have called them"! (13:2) This wasn't God the Father, nor God the Son, but God the Holy Spirit. The simple point to remember is that it was the Holy Spirit who called, separated, and empowered these men to minister.

Next, read Matthew 28:18-20—"Then Jesus came to them and said, 'All authority in heaven and on earth has been given to me. Therefore go and make disciples of all nations, baptizing them in the *name* of the *Father* and of the *Son* and of the *Holy Spirit*, and teaching them to obey everything I have commanded you. And surely I will be with you always, to the very end of the age."

The term, "name," is significant (28:19). Since there is only one God (singular), baptism is in the *name* (singular) of the Father, Son, and Holy Spirit. It is important to point out that the Father is a person, that the Son is a person, and that the Holy Spirit is also a person, and that all three persons of the Godhead share equal status in one's baptism experience. They are not two persons and an "it." There is *one* God who has chosen to reveal Himself as three persons.

Next, share John 14:16-17—"And I will ask the Father, and He will give you another Counselor to be with you forever— the Spirit of truth. The world cannot accept Him, because it neither sees him nor knows him. But you know him, for he lives with you and will be in you."

In this passage, Jesus repeatedly calls the Holy Spirit a person. He refers to the Spirit as "him." He is an *eternal* person, who can be known, and who will live *in* believers forever. He takes the form of Spirit both because it is His nature (God is Spirit—John 4:24) and because He desires to "work in you," to accomplish "His good pleasure" (Phil. 2:13).

Finally, look at John 14:26—"But the Counselor, the Holy Spirit, whom the Father will send in my name, will teach you all things and will remind you of everything I have said to you." Jesus again refers to the Holy Spirit as a person and One who will *teach* believers the things of God. Only a person can do that!

The Father Is God

If there is any question concerning the fatherhood of God, share these verses with your non-Trinitarian friend. First, show him that the Lord Jesus called Him both God and Father in His discussion about the value of spiritual food and physical food. "Do not work for the food which perishes, but for the food which endures to eternal life, which the Son of Man shall give to you, for on Him the *Father,* even *God* has set His seal" (NASB).

Next, refer to Paul's prayer request in Ephesians 1:17—"I keep asking that the God of our Lord Jesus Christ, the glorious Father, may give you the Spirit of wisdom and revelation, so that you may know him better." If necessary, continue by reading 2 Corinthians 1:3—"Praise be to the God and Father of our Lord Jesus Christ, the Father of compassion and the God of all comfort." Explain that God sovereignly chose to reveal Himself to us as a Father. It was He who said concerning Jesus, ". . . I will be a Father to Him, and He will be a Son to Me" (Heb. 1:5 NASB).

To help him see that God the Father and God the Son are one, show him Isaiah 9:6. "For a *child* will be born to us, . . . His name will be called Wonderful Counselor, Mighty God, *Eternal Father,* Prince of Peace" (NASB). Again the Father equals the Son and the Son equals the Father. There is only one God, but there are three persons called God in the Bible. The Trinity is the way God is, . . . "and without faith it is impossible to please Him, for he who comes to God must believe that He is and that He is a rewarder of those who seek Him" (Heb. 11:6 NASB). If a person rejects the Trinity, it is because he wants to comprehend rather than believe. Fortunately, salvation comes by faith, not comprehension.

Now briefly review the original statement of purpose. At this point, you have carefully and honestly demonstrated each truth concerning what the Bible teaches about the Trinity.

The Resurrection Powerfully Demonstrates the Trinity

The writings of both Luke and Paul bear witness to the fact that it was God who made the Resurrection possible.

"We are witnesses of everything he (Jesus) did in the country of the Jews and in Jerusalem. They killed him by hanging him on a tree, *but God raised him from the dead* on the third day and caused him to be seen" (Acts 10:39-40). In Paul's letter to the Romans, he explained conversion, saying, ". . . if you confess with your mouth, 'Jesus is Lord,' and believe in your heart that God raised him from the dead, you will be saved" (Rom. 10:9).

(1) *God the Father* raised the Son from the dead. In writing to the Thessalonians, Paul tells of their testimony: ". . . you turned to God from idols to serve the living and true God, and to wait for *his Son* from heaven, *whom he raised* from the dead—Jesus, who rescues us from the coming wrath" (1 Thess. 1:9-10). Who has a son? Only a Father. And who raised Him from the dead? It was God.

(2) *God the Spirit* raised the Son from the dead. "And if the *Spirit of him* who raised Jesus from the dead is living in you, he who raised Christ from the dead will also give life to your mortal bodies . . ." (Rom. 8:11).

(3) *God the Son* raised Himself from the dead. "Jesus answered them, 'Destroy this temple, and I will raise it again in three days.' The Jews replied, 'It has taken forty-six years to build this temple, and you are going to raise it in three days?' But the temple he had spoken of was his *body.* After he was raised from the dead, his disciples recalled what he had said. Then they believed the Scripture and the words that Jesus had spoken" (John 2:19-22).

Jesus' claim to divinity was nowhere more clearly enunciated than in His prophecy that He would raise His own body from the grave—and He even predicted that the miracle would occur three days after His death!

In summary, the Bible teaches that God raised Christ from the dead and proceeds to credit each of the Persons of the Trinity with history's greatest miracle. Ultimately, our non-Trinitarian friends who are honest must exercise their faith and accept the biblical doctrine of the Trinity.

Witnessing Helps for Dealing with non-Trinitarians

1. Frequently I have found that the question of Jesus' eternal pre-existence will be raised. Occasionally, a person will suggest that the term, "first-born of all creation," found in Colossians 1:15 implies that Jesus Christ was created at some time in the distant past by God the Father. This doctrine is nowhere taught in Scripture and can only be arrived at through a misinterpretation of this and other verses using the term, *first-born.*

The term, *first-born* (Col. 1:15, 18) refers to the preeminence of God who became visible to us as a man in the person of Christ. The passage is dealing with the divinity of Jesus Christ in His manhood, and this immediately causes problems for many non-Trinitarians. The true meaning of the term is expressed at the end of the passage in that He is "to have first place in everything" (1:18).

This may be illustrated by a term used in the United States. When the wife of the president is referred to as "the first lady of the land," this is not to say that she was the first woman ever born or created in her country. It simply means that of all the women in the United States, she fills the most *honored* position.

2. Jehovah's Witnesses will often attempt to take advantage of the biblical ignorance of new or uninformed Christians by asserting that the Hebrew word that is translated "LORD" (upper case) refers to Jehovah God, while the Hebrew word translated "Lord" (lower case) refers to Jesus Christ. They imply that the use of the lower case means that Jesus is a creation of God and therefore unequal with God. Through this highly simplistic argument, they seek to confuse new Christians in regard to the Trinity.

To help you give your Timothy a correct understanding in this matter, let me use an illustration. I am a man, but at the same time I possess a title and a personal name; therefore, I am called man, Reverend, and Billie Hanks, Jr. simultaneously. Linguistically, the same is true of our Creator.

He is *Elohim*, which is translated into English "God"; He has a title (Adonai), which is translated "Lord"; He has a personal name (Yahweh), which is translated "LORD"[1] (see Isa. 42:8).

---

[1]This technical difference between Lord and LORD is frequently explained in the front of study Bibles and has to do primarily with the tradition of the Jews in which they would not pronounce the personal name of God in their reading of the Scriptures (the Old Testament).

In Psalm 86, the psalmist says, "For you are great and do marvelous deeds; you alone are God. Teach me your way, O LORD, and I will walk in your truth; give me an undivided heart, that I may fear your name. I will praise you, O Lord my God, with all my heart; I will glorify your name forever" (vv. 10-12).

A. Notice that the psalmist says, "You alone are God" (v. 10).

B. Next he calls God, "LORD" (v. 11).

C. Then he calls God, "Lord" (v. 12).

D. In this passage, it is easy to demonstrate in context that both uses of capitalization refer to the same and only God.

3. To win an argument with a non-Trinitarian is not necessarily to win him to Christ. However, to lose an argument is assuredly not to win him to Christ. So try to know enough to win your arguments with non-Trinitarians. Do it graciously and kindly, but do it.

On my first trip to India, during my first sermon there, the head of the debate team at a university in Hyderabad was in the audience. I preached four times that afternoon, and he followed me to each location where I spoke. Finally, late that afternoon, he asked, "Could I have dinner with you? I'd like to talk with you about some of the things you have been saying." I replied, "Yes, would you be my guest for dinner this evening?"

He willingly agreed and came to the hotel where I was staying. He remained with me for a full eight hours, telling me in great detail about his concept of God. He was definitely unsettled about the divinity of Christ and the doctrine of the Trinity. Although influenced by Islam, he had drawn from several other sources in order to develop what he called his own personal religion. I said little or nothing for those eight hours. I just sat there and quietly listened as he talked incessantly.

Finally, in desperation, around 4:00 in the morning, I silently prayed, "Lord, what shall I do? I haven't gotten to tell him anything about You." In answer there came a spontaneous urging. So I looked straight at him and forcefully said, "Be quiet!"

He sat there, stunned.

I said, "Do you realize that it's 4:00 in the morning, and for eight hours you've been telling me what you believe? Now, for the next fifteen minutes, it's my turn. Please don't say any-thing—just listen, and the truth will set you free."

I told him God is revealed in Jesus Christ, showed him the necessity of the cross, and explained God's purpose in salva-tion. Then I said, "Now, it's your turn to speak."

He said, "Why hasn't anybody ever explained these things to me before? This is what I have been looking for all my life!"

I wanted to say that probably no one had ever told him because they couldn't get a word in edgewise!

Within the hour, he received Christ as his Savior and Lord, and soon after that he began to grow spiritually. Some time later, he married a Campus Crusade for Christ staff member, and I learned he was effectively using his debating and jour-nalistic skills for the gospel.

Whether in a cult or a world religion that has difficulty conceiving of the triune nature of God, a non-Trinitarian is almost always a religious person who has thought through his beliefs. The fact that he is God-conscious can be a significant asset in your efforts to help him in his search for the truth. You must be able to listen, evaluate, respond, and learn to dem-onstrate the verses that he needs to see.

Debate is not wrong. The apostle Paul used this method often in his ministry. So be willing to debate for the truth, but do so in an honest and respectful way.

Over 750 million non-Trinitarian monotheists currently in-habit our globe. These include Jews, Muslims, Jehovah's Wit-nesses, Mormons, Moonies, Unitarians, Jesus Only, and The Way International, plus other lesser-known groups, such as the Foundation of Yahweh. This means that every serious-minded Christian must resolve to be able to explain from the Scriptures the central doctrine of our faith. As you instruct your Timothy, practice sharing these verses with each other until they are a functional, inspirational part of your life.

11

Sharing Christ With Muslims

Due to increasing travel and world-wide shifts in population, it is no longer unusual to find followers of Islam in many traditionally-Christian parts of the world. Because of ancient rivalries, few religious groups have been more difficult to converse with on a meaningful spiritual level. Fortunately, however, those circumstances are now beginning to change.

Recently, during a trans-Atlantic flight, I enjoyed an excellent conversation and Bible study with a Muslim banker from London. Both his questions about Christ and his explanations concerning Islam were open and honest. This kind of experience is becoming more common with each passing year.

Perhaps because of misconceptions brought about by Muslim contact with Nestorianism,[1] it is sometimes necessary to assure our Islamic friends that Christians have always believed in one

---

[1] "We see an early exposure of Muhammad and his followers to a decadent, divided, and distorted Christianity. Islam arose in a religious milieux in which Christianity was riddled by the Christological controversy. The main Christian presence to which the early Muslims were exposed was the *community of Nestorians* —many of whom were slaves. They had dispersed from the Mediterranean region in the fifth century A.D. after their condemnation by one of the Church councils. They scattered migrating east to Persia and India and south to the Arabian peninsula. *They may be characterized as having been worldly and having a confused Christology.*" Dr. Earl R. Martin, *The Christian's Responsibility Toward Muslims.*

God—not three (God the Father, Mary the Mother of God, and Jesus the Son).[2] Typically, their questions concerning the Christian doctrine of the Trinity[3] and the divinity of Christ are unique to their religious background. For this reason, you will need to carefully teach your Timothy the information in this chapter in order to help prepare him for witnessing to Muslims.

Few men are as well qualified to give practical instruction in this area as Rev. Charles Marsh, a missionary to Muslim countries for forty-five years. His excellent book, *Share Your Faith With a Muslim,*[4] from which much of this chapter has been adapted, is a must for every Christian who desires to understand how to communicate the gospel to Muslim friends. Another excellent and more modern book is entitled, *Dialogue and Interfaith Witness with Muslims,* by Ray Register.[5]

The "ISA" of the Koran

Every Muslim professes to believe in Jesus, but we must understand what that really means. The "Isa" (Jesus) in the *Koran*[6]

---

[2]From *Share Your Faith With a Muslim,* by Charles R. Marsh. Copyright 1975. Moody Press. Moody Bible Institute of Chicago. Used by permission. p. 41.

[3]"For Muslims, the Christian doctrine of the Trinity amounts to Tritheism. Surah 4:141 'Say not "Trinity": desist: it will be better for you: For God is One God'." Martin.

[4]Marsh.

[5]Register, Ray G., Jr., *Dialogue and Interfaith Witness with Muslims.* Fort Washington, Pa: The World Evangelization Crusade, 1979.

[6]"The Koran is regarded as the perfect holy book of Islam, which supersedes all other scriptures. Islam shares in common with Christians certain revealed scriptures: Torah-The Pentateuch, Zabur-the Psalms, and Injil-The Gospel. These are the first three of the four holy books in Islam. The Koran is the fourth. The Bible is regarded by Muslims as being in a present corrupted form. They assert that Christians do not have the pure original revelation of God. They further claim that the Koran rectified distortions in Christianity brought about by Jesus' disciples—notably the Apostle Paul" (Martin).

is only one of the six great prophets of Islam. These are Adam, Noah, Abraham, Moses, Isa, and Muhammad. They see these men as major prophets, each of whom introduced a new law from God for his generation. In addition, some 124,000 lesser prophets are also revered.

The "Isa" of the *Koran* was sent only to the Jews. Though he was born of the virgin Mary, he was not the Son of God, and his teachings denied the doctrine of the Trinity. He healed the blind, cleansed lepers, and had the power to raise the dead, but this was only by God's permission. Rather than telling of the coming of the Holy Spirit, they believe he foretold the coming of Muhammad (see John 14:16).

The Muslim's "Isa" cursed Israel, was not crucified, and did not die—yet, he appeared to have died to those of his day. He is alive today and will return to earth to marry, have children, reign forty years, establish Islam worldwide, and die at Medina, where he will be buried in a special grave beside Muhammad.[7] In summary, the Koran specifically denies the two most outstanding truths about Christ in the Gospels: His *deity* and His *atoning death*.

Even a casual knowledge of biblical truth reveals that the "Isa" of the Koran is *not* to be equated with the Lord Jesus of the New Testament. For this reason, we must convey to the Muslim something of the true wonder of the person of our Lord before using the term, "Son of God," which refers to His deity. It will also be necessary to communicate "why" Jesus came and "why" He chose to die. Let us remember that until he grasps this truth, he cannot be saved (John 3:36). It will take time to fully communicate, but when one has done so, how rewarding it will be.[8]

Attempt to understand the Muslim point of view. Muslims believe "that the term, 'Son of God,' means that God had sexual intercourse with a woman and Jesus was born as a result.

---

[7]Marsh, p. 41.
[8]Marsh, p. 43.

This, they say, would be blasphemy!"[9] Because of *this*, Muslims genuinely feel that the name, "Son of God," is both dishonoring to God and to the Lord Jesus.

To deal with the deeper issue and lead them to a biblical understanding, we must emphasize the truth that if Jesus Christ were a *Savior* who was less than God, the bridge of salvation would be broken on God's end.

To *immediately* tell a Muslim that Jesus is "God" only widens the gap of misunderstanding. He may ask you, "When Jesus was born, was God born? When He died, did God die?" Because of his failure to understand the profound truth of the Trinity, he may then ask, "Who was looking after the world when God died for three days?"[10]

Communicating the Truth Concerning the Son of God

Lesson #1

When a Muslim asks, "Was Jesus the Son of God?" you can respond by asking, *"What do you understand the term, 'Son of God,' to mean?"*

He will probably reply, "It can have only one meaning: God went to bed with a woman, and a baby was born." Once he has stated his deep misconception, you can help him deal with it honestly.

"No Christian in all the world believes that; such a thought would be blasphemy!"

In astonishment, the Muslim may say, "Then, what does it mean?"[11]

You can then explain that in everyday speech the expression,

---

[9]Marsh, p. 42. Note: "Muslims do not accept Jesus Christ as the Son of God. They regard this idea as blasphemous. They say His Sonship is an invention of the Council of Nicea and that it is contrary to the basic tenet found in Surah 112:3 'He begetteth not, nor is He begotten' " (Martin).

[10]Marsh, p. 42.

[11]Marsh, pp. 42-43.

"son of," is used as a *metaphor* and does not imply a *physical* relationship. For example, a bad person is referred to as "the son of a jackal" in some countries, while in others a strong-willed person is called a "son of a gun." In the Bible, the apostles James and John are referred to as the "Sons of Thunder" (Mark 3:17). We know that jackals, guns, and thunder do not have human babies. The term, "son of," conveys the thought of likeness.[12] In the Bible, it describes a spiritual, rather than a physical, relationship.

This concept is clearly seen in the word, "image," which means "likeness." Colossians 1:15 says, "He is the image of the invisible God." The spiritual meaning intended by the term, "Son of God," is also expressed in Luke 1:35, "And the angel answered and said unto her, The Holy Ghost shall come upon thee, and the power of the Highest shall overshadow thee: therefore the Holy One which shall be born of thee shall be called the Son of God" (KJV). Here we can explain that it was His *sinless character, selfless love,* and *miraculous power* that marked His likeness to God.

Lesson #2

Moving beyond a casual witnessing conversation to a sustained relationship with a Muslim requires the patience to develop an environment of trust.

Like the experience of those in the day of Jesus' earthly ministry, there will ordinarily be progressive levels of understanding concerning the true meaning of His identity as the Christ. Pause to reflect. At first, those early believers recognized Him as a teacher, then as a healer, a prophet, and a Savior. Though He had said it many times in many ways, it was only after His death, burial, resurrection appearances, and ascension that they actually realized He was God. It should not seem strange to us that a modern-day Muslim would go through a similar process to find the truth.

---

[12]Marsh, p. 44.

It is good to remember that Muslims accuse Christians of making a *man* to be God. We must remind them that *the Bible consistently teaches it was God who became a man.* The eternal Word became flesh! The movement was from above, not from below. Jesus said, "You are of this world; I am not of this world" (John 8:23b). This important concept can be illustrated by other Scriptures, such as John 1:14a, which says, "And the Word was made flesh, and dwelt among us, and we beheld his glory . . ." (KJV).[13]

The Muslim often refers to Jesus Christ as the Word of God. Knowing that, you can read John 1:1-4 and affirm that God truly desires to speak to man. He does this through His Word. As an example of this, simply say, "Let me ask you a question. Where were the words I just spoke, before they came from my mouth? They were in my mind, but if you performed surgery on my brain, you would not find them. In some mysterious way, I and my words are the same. Whatever my words do, to please you or annoy you, you can accurately say that I am the one doing it. Just so, whatever the Word does, God Himself is actually doing it.[14] Jesus Christ did not merely speak about God, as other prophets did—He was God's sinless, perfect Word.

Lesson #3

In sharing your faith with a Muslim, you may begin by asking, *"What do you think about the person of Jesus Christ?"* As you talk, help him realize the importance attached to his answer. You can say, "One day Jesus Christ will return, and when He does, He will ask you the question that He once asked the Pharisees: 'What is your opinion of Me?' "

As you continue your conversation, you can say something like this: "Do you really feel that the Lord Jesus is just a prophet,

---

[13]Marsh, p. 43.
[14]Marsh, p. 44.

or one good man among many? No, He is unique. There is no one like Him in the world."[15]

To illustrate the uniqueness of Christ, the following questions from a penetrating message by Charles Marsh can be discussed. Although these questions may at first seem unnatural to you, you will find them to be effective in witnessing to a Muslim. Carefully discuss each question and answer with your Timothy. Be sure he is able to reconstruct the major points of this valuable presentation. To improve his skills, have him practice by asking these questions and giving the suggested answers.

Question #1: What do you think of the Lord Jesus' wonderful birth?

After the Muslim's response, point out that no one was ever born in the way Jesus was.

"Now the birth of Jesus Christ was as follows. When His mother Mary had been betrothed to Joseph, *before* they came together she was found to be with child by the Holy Spirit. And Joseph her husband, being a righteous man, and not wanting to disgrace her, desired to put her away secretly. But when he had considered this, behold, an angel of the Lord appeared to him in a dream, saying, 'Joseph, son of David, do not be afraid to take Mary as your wife; for that which has been conceived in her is *of the Holy Spirit*' " (Matt. 1:18-20 NASB). Seven hundred years before Jesus' miraculous birth, the prophet Isaiah foretold how He would be born (Isa. 7:14), and it happened exactly as he said. No other birth ever occurred like this. Even His name implies its uniqueness.[16]

Jesus was the son of Mary; however, you call Ishmael the son of *Abraham*, John the son of *Zacharias*, Muhammad the son of *Abdullah*. All other men take the name of their father. Why did Jesus take His mother's name? Because He had *no*

---

[15]Marsh, p. 46.
[16]Marsh, p. 46.

earthly father. He was born of the virgin Mary, by the power of God, apart from the intervention of a man.[17]

Question #2: Why do you think He came into the world?

After waiting for the Muslim to respond, point out that God created Adam, our father, from clay. State that we are children of Adam, and so were the prophets. We were created from the earth, but the Lord Jesus came down from heaven. Though He took upon Himself a human body and became a man, He was, nevertheless, pure and clean—like the snow and rain, that come from above.

It is no wonder the Bible says that all other men "have sinned and fall short of the glory of God" (Rom. 3:23). We are from the earth and are infected with sin. It was His response to our need that led Him to come into the world. The Scriptures teach that "Christ Jesus came into the world to save sinners" (1 Tim. 1:15).

At this point in your discussion, you could use the following illustration:

One night while walking, two men fell into a deep pit. One man said to the other, "Help me! Get me out of this place!" The other replied, "How can I? I'm in the same fix you are!"

Both men were in the pit, so they couldn't help each other. Then they heard a voice from above, calling, "Take hold of this rope." The assistance they needed came from one who had not fallen into the pit. He was able to bring them help from above.

The *best* man among the prophets *could not save us from the pit of sin,* but Jesus did not inherit a sinful nature. He was not from the earth; He came from above. God sent down His angels from heaven to announce His miraculous birth: "And the angel said unto them, Fear not: for, behold, I bring you good tidings of great joy, which shall be to all people. For unto

---

[17]Ibid.

you is born this day in the city of David a Savior, which is Christ the Lord" (Luke 2:10-11, KJV). How wonderful![18]

Question #3: What do you think of His life?

"Every man who fears God must confess his sin and ask forgiveness. David did. Abraham did."[19] In fact, one prophet said that he had to ask forgiveness of God seventy times a day. "(This was Muhammad, but do not mention his name.)"[20]

The Lord Jesus was perfect. You can search the Bible and the Koran in vain to find a single verse where Jesus asked for forgiveness. He did not *need* pardon, because He was sinless. Even those who knew Him best—his constant companions— said that He was without sin throughout His life.

God forgave the prophets when they confessed their sin, but Jesus was different. He could even say to His enemies: "Which of you can silence Me by pointing out one sin that I have done?" (John 8:46, Arabic) None of them could point out a single sin in His life. Who of us would dare to make such a challenge to our enemies?

During Jesus' trial, He was brought before Pilate and falsely accused. When Pilate could find nothing wrong, he washed His hands and said, "I am innocent of the blood of this just man."

There was never anyone else who was sinless. The quality of His life was unique and incomparable. No one in history was like Him.[21]

Question #4: What do you think about the teachings of the Lord Jesus?

On one occasion, His enemies sent the police to arrest Him. They listened to His teaching and then came back without

---

[18]Ibid., pp. 46-47.
[19]Ibid., p. 47.
[20]Ibid.
[21]Ibid.

having made the arrest, saying in amazement, "Never did a man speak the way this man speaks" (John 7:46 NASB).

Think about the meaning of Jesus' words: "I am the light of the world; he who follows Me shall not walk in the darkness, but shall have the light of life" (John 8:12 NASB).

A wise old man once explained what Jesus meant by using an illustration from nature. He said, "The prophets are like the moon. Just as the moon shines in the night, the prophets brought God's light to this poor, dark world. The crescent moon shines brighter and brighter, until it becomes a full moon, and then wanes and dies. But another full moon will come and take its place. So the prophets came, one after the other. Each one gave his message, died, and left his place to another."

Every nation has had some light from God. Men's religions are like the light of a candle or the moon. But who uses lesser lights when the sun has risen? Jesus said, "I am the light of the world." He is the sun of righteousness. Have you ever seen the sun wane or grow smaller? No, it never dies; it is for everyone in every land. Jesus Christ is like the sun. His teachings are for every country.[22]

Question #5: What do you think about His ability to meet needs?

He said, "I *am* the way, the truth, and the life." "The prophets all came to *point* the way back to God. They said, 'This is God's way. Do this. Do that. Follow this teaching. Keep the commandments.' But Jesus alone said, 'I *am* the way. Follow Me.' "[23]

One day, while visiting a large city, a little boy got lost. He asked a policeman to tell him the way home. The policeman tried to help by explaining: "Go up Grande Avenue, make the second turn to the left, then the third to the right. Cross the bridge, avoid the traffic circle, and take the middle road." The

---

[22]Ibid., pp. 36, 48.
[23]Ibid., p. 48.

little boy burst into tears. The policeman had given him the right directions, but the boy was incapable of following them. Just then a strong but kind man from the boy's home town came along. The boy was so tired, he could no longer walk, so the man actually picked him up and carried him home. The policeman told him the way, but the second man *was* his way. Only Jesus said, "I *am* the way."[24]

Question #6: What do you think about Jesus' knowledge?

Do you know *where* you will die? At home, or in a foreign country? Do you know *how* you will die? Will it be through illness, an accident, or natural death? Will you be old or young? Do you know the month or the day? You and I must admit that we do not know these things. Only God knows.

However, the Lord Jesus foretold where He would die. He even shared many details concerning His future death in Jerusalem. "And He took the twelve aside and said to them, 'Behold, we are going up to Jerusalem, and all things which are written through the prophets about the Son of Man will be accomplished. For He will be delivered to the Gentiles, and will be mocked and mistreated and spit upon, and after they have scourged Him, they will kill Him; and the third day He will rise again' " (Luke 18:31-33 NASB). He told His disciples *when* He would die. It would occur on the feast day when everyone would be killing a lamb to celebrate the Passover. He would die as the Lamb of God to take away the sin of the world. He explained that after three days He would rise again! Each event happened exactly as He predicted. He was not like other men. The prophets did not know the details surrounding their death, and neither do you or I.

The Lord Jesus alone could say, "No one (takes my life) away from Me, but I lay it down on My own initiative. I have authority to lay it down, and I have authority to take it up

---

[24]Ibid., pp. 48-49.

again" (John 10:18 NASB). He had never sinned and did not deserve to die. He could have gone to heaven without dying, but He *chose* to die for the sake of others. He gave His life for us, that we might be forgiven. He died as the Good Shepherd, giving His life for His sheep. His knowledge and courage were without equal. [25]

Question #7: *What do you think of His victory over death?*

After Jesus died, He was buried in a tomb in Jerusalem. Roman soldiers did their best to keep Him in the tomb. They rolled a huge stone across the entrance to the grave and then sealed it. Then they surrounded the grave with armed guards. Though they knew He was dead, they feared because of His prophecy that He would miraculously arise from the dead. As prophesied, angels came, and as He promised, He arose, showing Himself to His disciples on several occasions and then, finally, to more than 500 people. He rose again as He said He would. The resurrection took place to show everyone in the world that the saving work of God on the cross had been completed. The people saw Him, touched Him, and even ate and drank with Him, after His resurrection. He wanted them to fully believe that His words concerning His death and resurrection were true—so He showed them His hands, His feet, and His side!

For ordinary men, death is life's greatest enemy. The prophets died and remain dead. One day soon, you and I will also die, but the Lord Jesus conquered death! He is alive today! He has the power to save all of us who will come to God through Him. "Jesus said, 'I am the way, and the truth, and the life; no one comes to the Father, but through Me' " (John 14:6 NASB). He desires to make us pure and godly like Himself. He has prepared a place in heaven for all those who will believe in Him and accept His gift of salvation. "In my Father's house

---

[25]Ibid., pp. 50-51.

are many mansions; if it were not so, I would have told you. I go to prepare a place for you" (John 14:2 KJV).

What prophet is living today after having died? In all the world, He stands alone as the Savior. Is Jesus not totally unique?[26]

Question #8: What do you think of His ascension?

The Scriptures record that Jesus had just concluded His parting words to His faithful followers when He was lifted up from the earth and received into a cloud. As they were looking intently into the sky, two angels in white clothing said to them, "This Jesus, who has been taken up from you into heaven, will come in just the same way as you have watched Him go into heaven" (Acts 1:9-11 NASB). Because the Lord Jesus humbled Himself on our behalf and accepted an undeserved death out of love for us, the Scripture says that "God highly exalted Him, and bestowed on Him the name which is above every name, that at the name of Jesus every knee should bow, of those who are in heaven, and on earth, and under the earth, and that every tongue should confess that Jesus Christ is Lord, to the glory of God the Father" (Phil. 2:9-11 NASB). When Jesus ascended back to the glory of heaven, it was a fulfillment of the request included in His prayer: "And now, glorify thou me together with thyself, Father, with the glory which I had with thee before the world was" (John 17:5 KJV).

If I were to ask my Jewish friends whom they would like to have occupy the highest place of honor in heaven, they would probably say, "Moses." If I would ask the same question of my Muslim friends, they would probably say, "Muhammad"; and if I presented that same question to a group of Christians, they would doubtlessly say, "Jesus." However, God did not choose to consult with Jews, Muslims, Christians, or the followers of any other faith. For His own reasons, in His own time, He

---

[26]Ibid., pp. 51-52.

elected to exalt the Lord Jesus far beyond anyone in heaven or on earth. He is unique among men of every age and nation. This is God's sovereign choice, and even the proudest knee will ultimately bow to Him—either in heaven or on earth.[27]

Question #9: What do you think about His demands on your life?

The Lord Jesus said, "If anyone wishes to come after Me, let him deny himself, and take up his cross daily, and follow Me . . . whoever loses his life for My sake, he is the one who will save it" (Luke 9:23, 24b NASB). It has never been easy to accept the lordship of Jesus. His first disciples were called upon to leave their homes, their parents, and their jobs to follow Him. For many, there was the humiliation of breaking family traditions and experiencing the loss of social status. Today, He calls on us to demonstrate our willingness to do the same.

To acknowledge Him as less than your Savior and one true Lord is not to acknowledge Him at all. Jesus said, "No one can serve two masters . . ." (Matt. 6:24). He expects from us no less than He gave—all. To merely accept Him as a teacher, a healer, or a prophet, is to belittle the uniqueness of His sacred mission. He came to be the Savior. He said, "(I have) come to seek and to save that which was lost" (Luke 19:10 NASB). The prophets who needed forgiveness could never be our Savior. It took One who came from above, untainted by sin, to take our place and experience the full judgment of God on our behalf. Because Jesus lived out His claim and showed us the love, power, and purity of God as none other, His demands are absolutely logical. His birth, His life, His miracles, His love, His death, His resurrection, His return to heaven, His teachings, and His eternal presence, call for man's deepest response. There is no one like Him in heaven or on earth. Should He not be the King and Lord of your life?[28]

---

[27]Ibid., p. 52.
[28]Ibid., p. 53.

As you discuss the insights of this chapter with your Timothy, help him to understand that no matter how clear and truthful his witness[29] may be, in the final analysis a man must choose to respond to the drawing power of the Spirit of God, who enables men to experience the miracle of conversion. As the Scriptures say, "No one can say, 'Jesus is Lord,' except by the Holy Spirit" (1 Cor. 12:3b).

As Christ is exalted and uplifted, people of every race and religious background will continue to be drawn to Him as they come to realize that "religion" is not an adequate means of forgiveness and salvation, but the incomparable Christ is!

---

[29]For additional witnessing suggestions, see Appendix 7.

Appendices

Appendix 1
Bridge Illustration

Romans 3:23
Romans 6:23
Hebrews 9:27
Romans 5:8
Ephesians 2:8-9
John 1:12

The Sinner's Prayer

1. Confession—"Lord Jesus, I am a sinner."
2. Contrition—"But I am sorry for my sins."
3. Repentance—"I want to turn from my sins; I am willing to begin a new life with Your help."
4. Invitation—"Lord Jesus, please come into my heart and life right now."
5. Consecration—"From this moment forward, my life belongs to You and You alone."
6. Dependence—"I will love You, serve You, and tell others about You, and trust You to live Your life through me."
7. Thanksgiving—"Thank You, Lord, for coming into my life and for forgiving my sins today."

Assurance—1 John 5:11-13.

Appendix 2

The Trinity

Concept Statement: If there is one God, and if there are *three persons* called God in the Bible, then *by faith* I must accept the Christian doctrine of the Trinity, even though my mind cannot fully *comprehend* how God can be one yet three in perfect harmony and completeness.

1. Deuteronomy 6:4—There is only one God, Jehovah.
2. Isaiah 43:10-11—He is the LORD and only Savior.
3. Isaiah 44:6—He is the *first* and the *last.*
4. Revelation 1:8—He is the Lord God Almighty, the Alpha and Omega.
5. Revelation 22:13, 16—Jesus is the *first* and the *last,* the Alpha and Omega, the Beginning and the End.
6. Revelation 1:17-18—The one God who was the *first* and the *last* died and rose again!
7. Hebrews 1:1, 2, 8—God the Father calls the Son, "God."
8. Acts 5:3-4—Peter calls the Holy Spirit, "God."
9. John 6:27—Jesus calls the Father, "God."

The Trinity Revealed in the Resurrection

1. Acts 10:39-40—God raised Christ from the dead.
2. 1 Thessalonians 1:10—God the Father raised the Son from the dead.
3. Romans 8:11—God the Spirit raised the Son from the dead.
4. John 2:19-22—God the Son raised Himself from the dead.

Appendix 3

The Question of Baptismal Regeneration

1. All become Christians the same way—baptized *by the Spirit* into one unified body (the Body of Christ), *at the moment of conversion.*
   a. 1 Cor. 12:13.
   b. John 1:12—This occurs when we personally believe in Christ and receive Him into our lives by faith.
2. The Spirit of God lives in the believer, and a Christian belongs to God by virtue of that fact—Romans 8:9-11.

Example: Gentiles at the home of Cornelius (Acts 10; 15:7-11).
Acts 10:43, 47-48—Holy Spirit fell on Gentiles at initial moment of belief in Christ, baptizing them into the Body of Christ. Then they were baptized in water *because* of their salvation experience.
Acts 15:7-11—We are saved in the same way as those Gentiles—by the Holy Spirit cleansing our hearts *when we place our faith in Christ.*

Example: The Philippian jailer (Acts 16:30-31).
This is the only place in the New Testament where the question, "What must I do to be saved?" is asked. Paul's answer: "Believe in the Lord Jesus."

Answers to Typical Misconceptions:

Titus 3:5—We are not saved by what *we* do, but by what the Holy Spirit does. Acts 2:37-38—The question of "What shall we do?" in this passage clearly relates to repentance, not salvation. The *devout* Jews (Acts 2:5) who asked, "What shall we do?" were already saved under the Abrahamic covenant, due to their *personal faith* in Jehovah and their anticipation of the coming of the Messiah.

The only baptism that Peter and the early Jewish believers understood was the baptism of repentance, which both John the Baptist and they themselves on behalf of Jesus had administered for several years prior to this event. The promise of the Holy Spirit as a separate gift from God apart from the moment of salvation is not *normative* in the New Testament; however, in this unique instance, some Jews were devout and immediately accepted Jesus as the Christ once they heard the facts of the gospel proclaimed in the power of the Holy Spirit. This explains why 3,000 so readily professed faith in Jesus as the Messiah on this occasion.

They were not being converted from a background of paganism or secularism to Christianity, like Cornelius' household, but rather from Judaism to *completed* Judaism. Had the Lord not said, "My sheep hear my voice, and I know them, and they follow me" (John 10:27)?

The test of true spirituality on the part of those believing Jews in Jerusalem, Judea, and many other countries, was their response to the gospel when at last they heard the claims of Christ. It is only natural that such individuals, previously saved under the Abrahamic covenant, would immediately respond to the truth when they heard it. Their unusual circumstance only lasted for a brief number of years. Gradually, this unique possibility came to a conclusion, *never* to be repeated in history.

Over the centuries since that time, God has given the gift of His Spirit simultaneously with the act of receiving Jesus Christ by faith. This continues to be His one, and fully adequate, means of providing spiritual rebirth in the lives of believers.

Appendix 4

The Question of the Holy Spirit's Baptism

A One-Time Experience

God enters a new convert's life through the baptism of the Holy Spirit, at the moment of salvation—John 3:5; Romans 8:9; 1 Corinthians 12:13a.

Multiple Fillings

Conditions for:
    Personal conversion—1 John 1:9
    Continually living by faith—Ephesians 5:17b-20
    The Holy Spirit's presence—He is within you—Philippians 2:13; 1 Corinthians 6:19

Spiritual Power Is Revealed

1. In a godly life
    Example: John the Baptist
    Luke 1:15-17
    John 10:4-42
    Matthew 11:11-14
2. In evangelism
    Acts 1:8
    Matthew 28:18-20

The Holy Spirit's Gifts Sovereignly Distributed

    1 Corinthians 12:11

Many well-meaning Christians have become deeply confused and divided over the question of the baptism of the Holy Spirit. A careful reading of Appendix 3 will explain why a first- and second-blessing theology, could easily, though mistakenly, be developed from verses like Acts 2:38-39. Help your Timothy by explaining the difference between the *completion* of the saved believers in Acts 2, and the *conversion* of the Gentile believers in Acts 10. To further eliminate the possibility for confusion, point out the fact that the Samaritans of Acts 8, and the former disciples of John the Baptist mentioned in Acts 19 already believed in Jehovah God and were looking forward to the coming of the Messiah. This condition existed before Philip and Paul preached about the messianic identity of Jesus. Therefore, as in the case of the 3,000, we see an Old Testament faith being completed, resulting in a second spiritual blessing, namely, receiving the eternal indwelling presence of the Holy Spirit.

Jesus described this in John 14:16-17, when He said, ". . . I will pray the Father, and he shall give you another Comforter, that he may abide with you forever; even the Spirit of truth; whom the world cannot receive, because it seeth him not, neither knoweth him: but ye know him; for he dwelleth with you, and shall be *in* you" (KJV).

The gentile conversion described in Acts 10 involved no second blessing. The salvation that came by faith was received simultaneously with the power and baptism of the Holy Spirit. *In the modern vernacular*, what is described as the "first and second blessing" was received as one blessing, not two. This is true because no one in the world has lived under the first covenant since the generation that was contemporaneous with Christ. After their death, it became impossible to receive the Holy Spirit as a second work of grace. There has been no baptism of the Holy Spirit apart from the normal gentile-type of experience these many centuries.

Be careful to instruct your Timothy to earnestly seek to be filled with the Holy Spirit on an hourly, daily basis. Teach him to relate both his spiritual fruits and the spiritual gifts to the control of the Holy Spirit in his Christian life.

You must be careful to clearly differentiate between the baptism of the Holy Spirit at conversion and the filling of the Holy Spirit as a lifestyle. Emphasize the fact that God has an exciting ministry for him to carry out (Eph. 2:10), and that the Lord will sovereignly choose the gifts He needs to perform that high calling (1 Cor. 12:11).

In summary, whether your Timothy be ordained or a layman, the Scriptures are clear that God desires and is working toward his being filled and equipped for fruitful service. Paul builds on that foundation in his subsequent comment in 1 Corinthians 14:1, when he says, "Follow after love, and desire spiritual gifts. . . ." We are perfectly safe as long as we are enthusiastically open to God and do not begin to seek a gift of our own choosing. When He selects a gift, we will not need to tarry, practice, agonize, or read books about it. No instruction is necessary to receive a gift, when it is actually given by God. This sound doctrine will spare your Timothy from an abundant variety of counterfeit gifts and experiences that are widely available today.

Appendix 5

Sharing Christ With Jewish Friends

1. Five Levels of Judaism:
   a. Religious
   b. Cultural
   c. Social
   d. Genealogical
   e. National
2. The Annas and Caiaphas Question:
   a. Luke 3:1-2[1]
   b. John 11:47-53[2]
   c. John 18:12-13[3]
   d. John 18:19-24[4]
   e. Matthew 27:20[5]
3. John the Baptist:
   a. Matthew 11:11[6]
   b. Luke 1:15[7]
4. Jesus Christ:
   a. John 1:29[8]
   b. John 4:25-26[9]
5. The Bridge Illustration (see Chapter 5).

---

[1]"In the fifteenth year of the reign of Tiberius Caesar . . . during the high priesthood of Annas and Caiaphas, the word of God came to John son of Zechariah in the desert."

[2]"Then the chief priests and the Pharisees called a meeting of the Sanhedrin. 'What are we accomplishing?' they asked. 'Here is this man per-

forming many miraculous signs. If we let him go on like this, everyone will believe in him, and then the Romans will come and take away both our place and our nation.'

"Then one of them, named Caiaphas, who was high priest that year, spoke up, 'You know nothing at all! You do not realize that it is better for you that one man die for the people than that the whole nation perish.'

"He did not say this on his own, but as high priest that year he prophesied that Jesus would die for the Jewish nation, and not only for that nation but also for the scattered children of God, to bring them together and make them one. So from that day on they plotted to take his life."

³"Then the detachment of soldiers with its commander and the Jewish officials arrested Jesus. They bound him and brought him first to Annas, who was the father-in-law of Caiaphas, the high priest that year."

⁴". . . the high priest questioned Jesus about his disciples and his teaching.

" 'I have spoken openly to the world,' Jesus replied. 'I always taught in synagogues or at the temple, where all the Jews come together. I said nothing in secret. Why question me? Ask those who heard me. Surely they know what I said.'

"When Jesus had said this, one of the officials nearby struck him in the face. 'Is that any way to answer the high priest?' he demanded.

" 'If I said something wrong,' Jesus replied, 'testify as to what is wrong. But if I spoke the truth, why did you strike me?' Then Annas sent him, still bound, to Caiaphas the high priest."

⁵"But the chief priests and the elders persuaded the multitudes to ask for Barabbas, and to put Jesus to death" (NASB).

⁶" 'Truly, I say to you, among those born of women there has not arisen anyone greater than John the Baptist . . . ' " (NASB).

⁷"For he will be great in the sight of the Lord, and he will drink no wine or liquor; and he will be filled with the Holy Spirit, while yet in his mother's womb" (NASB).

⁸"The next day he saw Jesus coming to him, and said, 'Behold, the Lamb of God who takes away the sin of the world!' "(NASB).

⁹"The woman said to Him, 'I know that Messiah is coming (He who is called Christ); when that One comes, He will declare all things to us.'

"Jesus said to her, 'I who speak to you am He' " (NASB).

Appendix 6

Suggestions for Witnessing to Muslims
by Carl Ellis

For those who sense God's calling to minister to Muslims, here are some practical suggestions:

—Be yourself.

—Try to understand Islamic doctrine from the perspective of Islam. Recognize the corruption of Christianity Muhammad had encountered and that his motivation was to reform the worship of the one true God.

—Be a good listener. Don't evaluate a Muslim only on the basis of his doctrine. Examine the situation that led him to Islam and the goals he is trying to achieve through it.

—When the motivation and goals are biblical, affirm them. When they are not, lovingly challenge them. And whenever possible, use words according to his definitions, not yours.

—When dealing with a Muslim's doctrine, do not use the occasion to show him how much you know about his faith.

Instead, deal with him on the basis of what he expresses to you about his beliefs. You'll find he is never totally consistent with the doctrine he holds.

—It's always important to draw out the person by asking questions in the genuine spirit of wanting to be informed. Give him a chance to express himself, and make sure he knows you understand what he's saying.

Ask him, *"Is this what you mean?"* Then try to summarize his point. If he says, "Yes," then proceed to evaluate, critique, or challenge.

As in playing tennis, allow him to give you his best shot; then gently lob the ball back to his side of the net. Let him make the mistakes; then move in with your game plan.

In other words, do not be bowled over by his argument. Stand firm, with poise and confidence.

Remember, just as there is jailhouse religion among professing Christians, there will be the same among professing Muslims. Things are not always what they seem.

If you are familiar with his theology, you can tell when he begins to feel the pinch. Usually, he will begin to repeat himself or make up his theology on the spot.

Don't take advantage of his vulnerability by lording it over him. Rather, seek to communicate subtly but clearly that you are aware of his tenuous position. The very fact that you refuse to pulverize him will communicate more about the validity of the Christian faith than if you had devastated him with your rational arguments.

—Do not use a King James Bible. According to the teachings of some Muslim sects, King James himself translated this version and corrupted it. I recommend the New International Version.

—Avoid all pictures of God, Jesus, or any biblical characters, whether they be blue-eyed with blond hair or brown-eyed with Afros.

—Although in most cases the Muslim community may be a *de facto* black group, do not initiate issues concerning race. Many Muslims have a humanistic slant and see themselves beyond blackness. According to their humanistic claims, therefore, being black or white should not pose barriers.

—Never use the word *trinity.* Because of the Muslim's teaching, this word often connotes the worship of three gods and will bog you down with issues of polytheism.

From Scripture, we know that God's oneness of being is never diminished by His tri-personhood. There are many ways to express the Trinity concept. One way, for example, is to use the term *Godhead.*

—Don't be offended by the Muslim's use of the term *Allah*— it's simply the Arabic word for God.

—In dealing with Muslims, remove all offenses—except the cross. Against love, there is no defense, Islamic or otherwise.